系列总主编：张敬源

普通学术英语教程
听说与思考

English for General Academic Purposes
Listening, Speaking and Critical Thinking

总主编　都建颖
主　编　李伟平　彭启敏
编　者　都建颖　周超英　彭启敏　李伟平

图书在版编目(CIP)数据

普通学术英语教程:听说与思考/都建颖总主编.—北京:北京大学出版社,2013.7
(大学英语立体化网络化创新系列教材)
ISBN 978-7-301-22829-6

Ⅰ.普… Ⅱ.都… Ⅲ.学术交流—英语—听说教学—高等学校—教材 Ⅳ.H31

中国版本图书馆CIP数据核字(2013)第154156号

书　　　名:普通学术英语教程——听说与思考
著作责任者:都建颖　总主编
组 稿 编 辑:万晶晶
责 任 编 辑:黄瑞明
标 准 书 号:ISBN 978-7-301-22829-6/H·3342
出 版 发 行:北京大学出版社
地　　　址:北京市海淀区成府路205号　100871
网　　　址:http://www.pup.cn　新浪官方微博:@北京大学出版社
电 子 信 箱:zpup@pup.pku.edu.cn
电　　　话:邮购部 62752015　发行部 62750672　编辑部 62754382　出版部 62754962
印　刷　者:北京大学印刷厂
经　销　者:新华书店
　　　　　　787毫米×1092毫米　16开本　6.75印张　180千字
　　　　　　2013年7月第1版　2015年5月第2次印刷
定　　　价:25.00元

未经许可,不得以任何方式复制或抄袭本书之部分或全部内容。
版权所有,侵权必究
举报电话: 010-62752024　电子信箱: fd@pup.pku.edu.cn

前　言

本书主要目的：
　　1. 强化学术讲座、小组讨论、研究成果展示等学术活动要求的基本听说技能，主要包括如何聆听对方的讲话，辨别和记录要点，如何参与小组讨论，如何通过演讲与答辩进行成果展示和信息交流。
　　2. 培养批判性思维能力，这是高等教育的主要目的，对专业学习和个人素质提高都具有重要意义。批判性思维能力主要包括认清事实、发现问题、寻找并考量解决方案等能力。
　　3. 提高对问题的识别、分析和判断能力，以及口头表达能力，包括表达的正确性、流畅性、充分性、有效性和完整性。

本书编写原则：
　　1. 注意过渡性。本书以综合性大学本科一、二年级学生为对象，在材料选择、练习设计、章节组织上既体现了英语学习从高中向大学阶段的过渡，又照顾到大多数学生的接受程度和进一步发展的实际需求，难度适中，多以例子分析代替刻板的理论输入。
　　2. 以听促说，并与读写结合。本书以培养学生的学术口语表达能力为主要目标，并配以影音材料。这些材料服务于两个目的，第一，为学生提供以学术讲座、小组讨论等情境中的学术口语表达的思维架构和语言表达范本；第二，培养学生对问题的识别、分析、总结和判断能力，从而最终做到能"理性地思考，清晰地表达"。

词汇把控：
　　本书在编写和选取材料时以普通学术英语为目的，尽量避免使用专业术语、口语以及冷僻的词汇和表达方式。学生在本课程结束时词汇量应达到3500至4000，其中主要是普通学术英语词汇（基本词汇750，扩展词汇2500）。

编撰指导思想：
　　学术英语听说与读写联系密切，听与读是信息输入过程，说与写是信息输出过程，两个过程都以搜索信息和审慎思考为基础，并借助各种语言技巧，达到有效交流的目的。因此，学术英语教学既注重思维方式的培养，也注重语言表达的得体与严谨。目前我国高校大多数本科新生仍然认为英语学习主要是高级词汇和复杂句子的堆砌，而在具体表达时缺乏逻辑性、分析性和批判性。而大多数英语教师对学术英语教学也存在误解，认为学术英语强调专业词汇和文章体例。通过本书的撰写，我们希望大学英语课堂能培养学生思辨能力，提高语言能力，从而增强学生的整体素质，在国际交流中体现中国大学生的真正风采。

目 录

Unit One	**The X Factor for Success**	1
Part I	Significance of Pre-Listening Work	2
	Reading Text 1 John Dewey: A Philosopher and Democratic Educationist	3
	Reading Text 2 When Lei Feng Meets Non-believers	5
Part II	Effective Pre-Listening Strategies	7
Part III	Micro-Skills: Communicating Orally in Academic Situations	16
Part IV	Recycling	21
Unit Two	**Justice**	23
Part I	Significance of Identifying Key Ideas	24
	Reading Text 1 Gay Marriage "Unnatural"	24
	Reading Text 2 Equal Treatment Is Real Issue—Not Marriage	26
Part II	Distinguishing the Main Idea from the Detail	27
Part III	Micro-Skills: Word Families	32
Part IV	Recycling	34
Unit Three	**How It's Made**	36
Part I	About Taking Notes in Lectures	37
	Reading Text Technological Advances: Discovery, Invention, Innovation, Diffusion	39
Part II	Notes on a Process	42
Part III	Micro-Skills: Understanding Sentence Stress	47
Part IV	Recycling	49
Unit Four	**Health and Fitness**	52
Part I	Listen Actively	53
	Live-expectancy Quiz How Long Will You Live	55
Part II	Digression	57

1

| Part III | Micro-Skills: General Academic Words in Lectures | 62 |
| Part IV | Recycling | 65 |

Unit Five Globalization 68
Part I	Introduction of New Terminologies	69
	Reading Text Globalization: Don't Worry, Be Happy	69
Part II	Recognizing Signals of Definition	71
Part III	Micro-Skills: Weak Forms of Function Words	77
Part IV	Recycling	79

Unit Six Let's Put Birth Control Back on the Agenda 81
Part I	What Lecturers Do in Lectures?	82
	Reading Text Birth Control for Men? For Real This Time?	84
Part II	Structure Analysis of a Lecture	87
Part III	Micro-Skills: Common Expressions in Lectures	93
Part IV	Recycling	96

Unit One
The X Factor for Success

Pre-listening Strategies

Lead-in Questions

1. What do you usually do before listening activities?
2. What do we need to do when we are given heroic figures as role models?

1

Part I Significance of Pre-Listening Work

1.1 Why do pre-listening work?

In real life, when we listen to an interview of a famous person, we probably have known something about that person already. When we choose to listen to a lecture out of our personal or professional interest, we probably know which topic is being discussed. For native speakers and listeners, it is unusual to listen to something without having some idea of what they are going to hear.

In our first language we rarely have trouble understanding what we are listening. But, in a second language, it is one of the harder skills to develop—dealing at speed with unfamiliar sounds, words and structures. This is even more difficult if we do not know the topic under discussion, or who is speaking to whom. Therefore, it is significant for second-language learners to do pre-listening work.

1.2 Advantages of pre-listening work

Pre-listening work helps us to generate interest, build confidence, make clear the purpose of listening, focus on the useful information, and facilitate listening comprehension.

The following are two articles about heroic figures. When people in modern society are overwhelmed by heroic figures in fields like economics, sports, high technology, and maybe warfare, few would spare time pondering on people whose thoughts and behavior were highly politically and philosophically influential. The articles present two heroic figures: John Dewey and Lei Feng. They both impact on the Chinese education, but in largely different ways. Discuss in groups about what you know about the two figures: their life, major work, social influence, anecdotes and your evaluations about them. Then read the articles, check whether the ideas expressed in the articles meet your anticipations. Think about whether your discussion contributes to your reading comprehension, and in what ways it does so.

Unit One The X Factor for Success

Reading Text 1

John Dewey: A Philosopher and Democratic Educationist

1 John Dewey (1859—1952) was an American philosopher, psychologist, and educational reformer whose ideas have been influential in education and social reform. Dewey was an important early developer of the philosophy of pragmatism and one of the founders of functional psychology. He was a major representative of progressive education and liberalism. Although Dewey is known best for his publications concerning education, he also wrote about many other topics, including experience, nature, art, logic, inquiry, democracy, and ethics.

2 In 1919, while traveling in Japan on sabbatical leave, Dewey was invited by Peking University to visit China, probably at the request of his former students, Hu Shi and Jiang Menglin. The Chinese students' demonstrations on May Fourth excited and energized Dewey, and he ended up staying in China for two years, leaving in July 1921.

3 In these two years Dewey gave nearly two hundred lectures to Chinese audiences and wrote nearly monthly articles for Americans in *The New Republic* and other magazines. Dewey advocated that Americans support China's transformation and that Chinese base this transformation in education and social reforms, not revolution. Hundreds and sometimes thousands of people attended the lectures, which were interpreted by Hu Shi. For these audiences, Dewey represented "Mr. Democracy" and "Mr. Science," the two personifications which they thought represent modern values and replace "Mr. Confucius," the representative of traditional culture. Perhaps Dewey's biggest impact, however, was on the forces for progressive education in China, such as Hu Shi and Jiang Menglin, who had studied with him, and Tao Xingzhi, who had studied at Columbia School of Education.

4 While Dewey's educational theories have enjoyed a broad popularity during his lifetime and after, they have a troubled history of implementation. Dewey's writings can

also be difficult to read. And his tendency to reuse commonplace words and phrases to express extremely complex reinterpretations of them makes him susceptible to misunderstanding. So while he held the role of a leading public intellectual, he was often misinterpreted, even by fellow academics. Many enthusiastically embraced what they mistook for Dewey's philosophy, but which in fact bore little resemblance to it.

5   Dewey tried, on occasion, to correct such misguided enthusiasm, but with little success. Simultaneously, other progressive educational theories, often influenced by Dewey but not directly derived from him, were also becoming popular, such as Educational perennialism which is teacher-centered as opposed to student-centered. The term "progressive education" grew to encompass numerous contradictory theories and practices. Several versions of progressive education succeeded in transforming the educational landscape: the guidance counseling, to name but one example, springs from the progressive period. Radical variations of educational progressivism were troubled and short-lived, a fact that supports some understandings of the notion of failure. But they were perhaps too rare and ill-funded to constitute a thorough test.

6   Dewey is considered the representative of liberalism by many historians, and sometimes was portrayed as "dangerously radical." Meanwhile, Dewey was critiqued strongly by American communists because he argued against Stalinism and had philosophical differences with Marx, despite identifying himself as a democratic socialist. Historians have examined his religious beliefs. Biographer Steven C. Rockefeller, traced Dewey's democratic convictions to his childhood attendance at the Congregational Church, with its strong proclamation of social ideals. However, historian Edward A. White suggested in *Science and Religion in American Thought* (1952) that Dewey's work had led to the 20th century rift between religion and science.

(Adapted from http://en.Wikipedia.org/wiki/John Dewey and http://en.wikipedia.org/wiki/Democracy_and_Education)

Unit One The X Factor for Success

Reading Text 2

When Lei Feng Meets Non-believers

1 Lei Feng, a household name since the 1960s, is known for devoting almost all of this spare time and money to selflessly helping the needy. Late Chairman Mao Zedong called on the entire nation to follow Lei's example one year after Lei's death in 1962. However, debates over whether Lei Feng's spirit, mainly altruism, dedication, patriotism and modesty, is out of date seem to have grown more heated in recent years. The following part of this article presents different ideas about this icon among the general public and the scholars.

2 "When Lei Feng died in the line of duty, he was only 22, but his short life gives concentrated expression to the noble ideas of a new generation, nurtured with communist spirit, and also to the noble moral integrity and values of the Chinese people in the new period. These are firm faith in communist ideals, political warm-heartedness for the Party and the socialist cause, the revolutionary will to work for self-improvement, the moral quality and self-cultivation of showing fraternal unity and taking pleasure in assisting others, the heroic spirit of being ready to take up responsibilities for a righteous cause without caring for one's own interest and safety, the attitude of seeking advancement, and the genuine spirit of matching words with deeds and eventually fulfilling one's duties." (Editorial, *People's Daily*, 5 March, 1993)

3 Chinese leaders have praised Lei Feng as the personification of altruism. Leaders who have written about Lei Feng include Deng Xiaoping, Zhou Enlai, and Jiang Zemin. His cultural importance is still reproduced and reinforced by the media and cultural apparatus of the Chinese government, including emphasizing the importance of moral character during Mao's era. Lei Feng's prominence in school textbooks has since declined, although he remains part of the national curriculum. The term "活雷锋"(literally "living Lei Feng") has become a noun (or adjective) for anyone who is seen as selfless, or anyone who goes out of

their way to help others.

4   Details of Lei Feng's life, as presented in the official propaganda campaign, have been subject to dispute among scholars. While someone named Lei Feng may have existed, scholars generally think the person depicted in the campaign was probably a fabrication. Some observers noted, for instance, that the campaign presented a collection of twelve photographs of Lei Feng performing good deeds. The photographs were of exceptionally high professional quality, and the depicted Lei—supposedly an obscure and unknown young man — engaging in mundane tasks.

5   The impossible details of Lei Feng's life according to official propaganda let him to become a subject of negation or ignorance among some Chinese people. A survey by Xinhua News Press in 2008 noted that a large number of elementary school students have vague knowledge of Lei Feng's life, despite the reasonable understanding of Lei's spirit.

(Adapted from http://en.wikipedia.org/wiki/Lei_Feng)

Finish Practice 1 about Steve Jobs, and discuss what kind of pre-listening work you can do.

Practice 1: Blank filling (course audio material 1.1)

Listen to the VOASE Report on Steve Jobs two times, complete the missing information and figure out which statement is fact (F) and which is opinion (O).

1) (_____) Steve Jobs died of _____ at the age of _____.

2) (_____) Steve Jobs' adopters (养父母) supported _____ in electronics.

3) (_____) Steve Jobs rejoined Apple in 1997 and he helped remake Apple from a business that was _____ then to _____ in the world today.

4) (_____) By making computers personal and putting the Internet in our pockets, he made the information revolution not only _____, but _____ and _____.

5) (_____) He died a day after the company released a new iPhone version that met with _____.

6) (_____) The fact that he was able to redesign American commerce top to bottom and across is really _____.

Unit One The X Factor for Success

Part II Effective Pre-Listening Strategies

2.1 What are pre-listening strategies?

Pre-listening work is guided by learning strategies. Strategies are the thoughts and behaviors that learners used to help them comprehend, learn, orretain information. There are three main types of strategies: metacognitive, cognitive and social/affectivestrategies. The metacognitive strategy was a kind of self-regulated learning. It included the attempt to plan, check, monitor, select, revise, and evaluate, etc. strategies.The cognitive strategies are related to comprehending and storing input in working memory or long-term memory for later retrieval.They are classified into bottom-up strategies andtop-down strategies. Social/affective strategies are the techniques listeners used to collaborate with others, to verify understanding or to lower anxiety. Strategies and the ability to use them effectively were particularly important in foreign language listening.

Pre-listening strategies, which are applied before listening process, belong to metacognitive strategy. The strategies include **checking the listening tasks, pre-learning relevant vocabulary, activating current knowledge, and predicting content** etc. For teachers, they should engage the learners in a pre-listening activity. This activity should establish the purpose of the listening activity and activate the schemata by encouraging the learners to think about and discuss what they already know about the content of the listening text. This activity can also provide the background needed for them to understand the text, and it can focus attention on what to listen for.

2.2 Pre-listening checklist

Several effective pre-listening strategies are listed as follows:
- Make clear your purpose of listening;
- Check the listening tasks if you need to finish exercises;
- Think about the lecture and the lecturer's purpose;

- Predict content, opinions, or key words of the lecture by activating prior knowledge and experience of language (prediction strategy);
- Pre-learn vocabulary relevant to the subject that you are likely to hear.

The following is a checklist for pre-listening performance.

Pre-listening Performance Checklist	
Before listening	**Yes**
I understand the task (what I have to do after I have finished listening).	
I know what I must pay attention to while I listen.	
I have asked the teacher for clarifications, if necessary.	
I have attempted to recall all that I know about the topic.	
I have attempted to recall what I know about the type of text I will listen to and the type of information I will probably hear.	
I have made predictions on what I am about to hear.	
I am ready to pay attention and concentrate on what I am about to hear.	
I have encouraged myself.	

(Place a check mark "√" in the "yes" column when verifying each statement)

In order to improve my performance, next time I will _____
_____
_____
_____

(The table is adapted from Mendelsohn (1994:94))

Unit One The X Factor for Success

Finish the following Practice 2, before listening, you need to: a. self-learn the word bank which relevant to the listening material; b. complete the Pre-listening Performance Checklist.

Word Bank (Practice 2):

multibillion-dollar	the Macintosh
insanely	prevail
abrasive	ouster
Pixar Studios	revitalize
Brim	pancreatic cancer
commencement address	Stanford University
decade	destination
undergo	liver transplant
CEO	the Silicon Valley

Practice 2: Listen to the NBC news of "Steve Jobs: Remembering a Genius"; with appropriate pre-listening strategies, finish the exercises. (course audio material 1.2.1~1.2.4)

Exercise 1: *Listen to the headline of the report and complete the following chart about the death of Steve Jobs. (course audio material 1.2.1)*

Cause of his death	Steve Jobs died of 1) _____ at the age of 2) _____.
Fame of Steve Jobs	3) _____; 4) _____; The man behind 5) _____.
Our celebration	We celebrate 6) _____, 7) _____ and 8) _____.

Exercise 2: *Listen to the Standout of the reporter, and then retell what is Steve Jobs based on the outline given below. (course audio material 1.2.2)*

This is a very sad day for 1) _____. They're mourning Steve Jobs, a man who 2) _____ and had no 3) _____ but 4) _____ and transformed 5) _____.

Exercise 3: *Listen to the News Story and then answer the following questions. (course audio material 1.2.3)*

1) According to the reporter, what's the secret of Steve Jobs' success?

2) Why did Steve Jobs think that the computer industry hasn't done a good job?

3) What are the 2 possible causes of Steve Jobs' ouster from Apple in 1985?

4) When did Steve Jobs return to Apple and what did he achieve?

5) Which product of Apple changed people's way of consuming media?

Unit One The X Factor for Success

Exercise 4: *Complete the following chart on Steve Jobs' declining health.(course audio material 1.2.4)*

Time	Incidents
2004	He was operated on for _____ ;
2009	He received _____ ;
08-24-2011	He stepped down _____ ;
10-05-2011	He died peacefully _____ .

2.3 Prediction strategy

Prediction, or looking ahead, is a basic strategy for using prior knowledge to understand a text. It is an activity learners carry out before listening to a lecture, where they predict what they are going to hear, generates a hypothesis about the type, purpose, or scope of a lecture. This gives them a reason to listen, as they confirm or reject their predictions.

We can take the following two steps to predict a lecture. **First**, look at the title of the lecture and any other clues you have (photos, maps, charts, outlines,etc.) and think of specific questions you think might be answered in the lecture.Then thinkabout possible answers to each of your questions. Discuss the questions with a partner, if possible. If you have trouble thinking of questions, consider the major question words (who, what, when, where, why, how) and ask yourself how they might apply to the lecture topic. Creating these "**prediction questions**" will help you maintain your focus during lectures. In addition, the answers to the questions you form during this pre-listening step will often correspond to the actual main ideas of the lecture; in this way, these questions actually improve comprehension by helping you to identify main ideas and discriminate them from less important details.

Second, try to predict vocabulary you may hear in the lecture. To do this, you can analyze the main words in the title of the lecture. A dictionary and the saurus will be very helpful.

For example:

Analysis Questions	Vocabulary
What are some phrases expressing "give a lecture"?	*make/give a speech, give a talk, make/give a presentation, deliver an address*
Who gives lectures? Who listens to them?	*lecturers, speakers, presenters, professors, teachers, politicians audience, students, colleagues, professionals, the general public*
Where do people give lectures?	*in universities/colleges/high schools, in front of a class, behind a podium, on a platform, on stage Advanced Listening*
What can a lecture contain?	*introduction, main points, details, conclusion stories, anecdotes*
Who are some famous lecturers or speakers?	*Winston Churchill, Franklin D. Roosevelt, Martin Luther King, Cicero*

You can use this prediction strategy **during the lecture** as well. That is, as often as you can, try to predict what kinds of information might come next. Even if some of your predictions are incorrect, this strategy will help you stay focused and give you a better chance of general comprehension.

While we are listening, semantic markers can help us to predict. Semantic markers are words and phrases that help signal the progression of ideas. Some useful semantic markers are listed as follows.

1. The markers used for listing:

    firstly, my next point is, last/ finally

2. The markers which show us the cause and effect relationship between one idea and another:

    so, therefore, since, thus (we see)

3. The markers which indicate the speaker is going to illustrate his ideas by giving examples:

    for instance, let's take, an example of this was ...

4. The markers that introduce an idea which runs against what has been said, or is going to be said:

    nevertheless, and yet, although, on the other hand

Unit One The X Factor for Success

5. The markers which indicate the speaker is about to sum up his message, or part of it:

   to summarize, it amounts to this, in other words, if I can just sum up, what I have been saying is this

6. The markers used to express a time relationship:

   then, previously, while, after that, when

7. The markers used to indicate the relative importance of something:

   it is worth noting, I would like to direct your attention to

8. The markers used to rephrase what has already been said, or to introduce a definition:

   in other words, let me put it this way, to put it another way, that is to say

9. The markers that express a condition:

   if, unless, assuming that

Now finish the following Practice 3. Before listening, you need to: a. self-learn the word bank; b. with the help of the title and any other clues you have, predict specific questions and think about possible answers, predict vocabulary; c. complete the Pre-listening Performance Checklist.

Word Bank (Practice 3):

retina display	FaceTime
blow away	sparkle
pixel	fuzzy
clarity	optical elimination
laminate	App
application	inbox
LED flash	incredible
custom designed	silicon

Practice 3: Listen to the episode about Apple iPhone 4 Design; with appropriate pre-listening strategies, finish the exercises. (course audio material 1.3)

Exercise 1: *Main idea dictation.*

Listen to the introduction of iPhone 4, and write down the main idea.

Exercise 2: *Complete the text with one word in each space. All the words are adjectives.*

In 2007, the iPhone re-invented the phone. In 2008, the iPhone 3G brought 1) _____ 3G networking, and 2) _____ app store. In 2009, the iPhone 3GS was twice as 3) _____ and brought out 4) _____ features like video recording. For 2010, the iPhone 4 is the 5) _____ forward since the 6) _____ iPhone. We are introducing the 7) _____ retina display（视网膜屏幕显示）. And, we are bringing video calling to the world. We call it Face Time. It's gonna change the way we communicate forever.

Exercise 3: *Watch the video from 5'36" to 6'13". Work with your partner to figure out the stunning features and functions of iPhone 4.*

1. 1) _____, 2) _____, 3) _____, ultimately, all of these become relevant when you just hold it in your hand.

2. Even if 4) _____ was the only new feature we were delivering, it has been an amazing new iPhone. But it is the fact that we get 5) _____, 6) _____, 7) _____, 8) _____, 9) _____, or 10) _____. These gonna change everything, all over again.

Unit One   The X Factor for Success

Exercise 4: *Complete the following chart about iPhone 4. Some of the information has been provided. It may be challenging to most of you, yet it will be highly rewarding.*

Features	Functions	Advantages
Face Time	It's all about 1) _____.	1. It switches from 2) _____ to 3) _____, so you can 4) _____. 2. It's so 5) _____ as your phone, you'll be able to 6) _____.
retina display	To provide you 7) _____, 8) _____ shapes in turn.	1. It's the 9) _____ ever built on iPhone. 2. At 326 pixels per inch, you get 10) _____ as before.
optical elimination	To add the sharp and 11) _____.	That's a very precise technical process that laminates cover glass to the display, and eliminate light refresh.
Apps	To show more details than you've ever seen on any device before.	1. Text: ... 2. Multitasking: ...
Mail	To make mailing efficient.	You can see 12) _____ in 13) _____. And it allows you to 14) _____ in 15) _____ by thread.
5M Camera		1. The LED flash enables you to take photos 16) _____. 2. The camera captures full 720P 17) _____ at up to 30 frames per second. 3. Not only can you 18) _____ great video, but you can also 19) _____ your video, right on your iPhone with iMovie.

Part III Micro-Skills: Communicating Orally in Academic Situations

There are a variety of situations where you need to express your opinions, clarify your standpoint, provide or ask for advices and suggestions. To achieve these purposes successfully requires not only appropriate language, but also a good understanding of academic culture and conventions, as well as the great intellectual investment. It is also important that you develop and shape your opinions and standpoints through active participation in discussions and presentations.

3.1 Discussion skills

For discussions, students mainly play two kinds of roles: providing one's own opinions as a member of the group, and/or summarizing the final outcome of the discussion as the group leader or reporter. As a group member, the student may:
- Listen to what others say, and ask them to clarify the meaning or provide explanation for better understanding;
- Build on others' opinions by adding his/her own ideas;
- Explains his/her opinion briefly and clearly;
- Make an effort to join the discussion in spite of nervousness and difficulty;
- Encourage others to speak by asking for suggestive solutions to specific problems, challenges, doubts.

Unit One   The X Factor for Success

Exercises: *The following is useful language used for discussion. Add as many other expressions as you can.*

Table 1: Language used for group member

Clarifying the meaning	So, what you are saying is ... If I understand you correctly, you mean ... I'm not sure if I followed you. Could you explain ... again, please?
Adding one's own idea	I partially (totally) agree with you on that ... It seems to me that ... From my perspective I would have to argue that ... I take your point, but ...
Explaining one's own viewpoint	The reason for me to say so is because ... My viewpoint is based on the fact that ... The theoretical (factual, statistic) support of my viewpoint comes from ...
Asking for opinions and suggestions	One thing that I couldn't understand is ... I have some difficulty in ... There are a few things that I would like to have your help. First, ...

The group leader takes more responsibilities in organizing the discussion, controlling the time, encouraging the participation, and probably reporting the outcome. It is very important for the chairperson to clarify the focus, main theme or the central task of the discussion. Therefore, in addition to providing his/her own opinion, the group leader may also have to be responsible for the following activities:

Table 2: Language used for group leader

Getting started	So, shall we begin? Is everyone clear about what we are going to do? Ok, we're going to look at the following issue/question/topic ... Who would like to be the first sharing with us his or her idea on ...?
Managing the time	Right, would anyone like to add more on ...? I am afraid we are a bit off the target. I suppose we should concentrate on ... What you said is interesting, but I am not sure if we should focus more on ... We seem to be running out of time. Can we move on to the next question ...?
Closing	So, we all agree on that ..., but at the same time, we have different opinions on ... Does anyone want to make a final point? Have we missed anything or has our discussion covered all the tasks? So, our conclusion is ...

> **Practice 4: Discussion practice**
> *Form a group with about five other students; discuss your understanding of Lei Feng as a heroic figure in China. You can present your opinion from any ONE particular aspect. It will be very helpful if you clarify this aspect at the very beginning of your talk.*

3.2 Presentation skills

When planning a presentation, you need a topic; you also need to find a focus within the topic. For example, a presentation on the topic of Lei Feng as a heroic figure in China can be focused on the definition of hero, or on the positive or negative influence of the hero, or both, etc. You then need to generate ideas around your focus; organize your ideas, ensuring your main points are highly relevant to your focus. The following are some sub-skills involved in presentation.

Unit One The X Factor for Success

Talk:
- Stick to the point: being carried away by irrelevant information will confuse the audience and make your presentation a failure.
- Be aware of the audience: remember your audience and make it easy for them to follow your talk.
- Be very aware of the time: finish the presentation within the given time; make sure you slow down for key opinions or information so that your audience has time to understand what you are presenting.
- Do not just read: try to express or emphasize the ideas and information in your own words.

Slides:
- Logical order: begin with overview or questions and end with conclusion or answers.
- Moderate number: count the time you are given for speech, and allocate the number of the slides accordingly.
- Readable content: make sure all the audience can see clearly what is written in the slide.
- Friendly layout: make sure your audience has sufficient support to understand the words and pictures used in the slides.

Being a witty answerer if not an elegant one:
- Provide a straight answer which is followed by brief explanations.
- Stay calm and courteous to rude askers.
- Be tactical in dealing with irrelevant questions (you could response by saying "this is an interesting question, but our immediate concern is ... However, it would be nice if ...")
- Honesty is always a virtue.

Some extra tips to reduce nervousness:
- Do rehearse to organize and time your talk.
- Get some water aside, you may need it when your mouth and throat are dry with nervousness.
- Smile to create a friendly and comfortable atmosphere.

- Confidence derives from the fact that you are more familiar with the topic of your presentation, and better prepared than your audience is.
- Talk low, talk slow and don't say too much because the academic presentation differs greatly from other public speech.

Presentation is a two-way communication. The speaker needs to be aware of the audience, and try to establish a clear understanding of key issues among the audience. Listeners, on the other hand, play an equally important role in the whole process of presentation. They need to listen carefully and actively. Being a careful listener helps one to understand the focus and key information presented by the speaker. Being an active listener requires the audience to think critically, take notes where necessary, and raise valuable questions, comments and suggestions for the follow-up discussion.

> **Practice 5: Making a presentation**
> There are many widespread quotations from Steve Jobs, such as "stay hungury, stay foolish," which may have inspired many young people. Of all the quotations you know, which one impresses you most? Think about it, make a presentation to share your views with the entire class.

Unit One The X Factor for Success

Part IV Recycling

4.1 Building your vocabulary

These are the 12 key vocabulary words and phrases for this unit. Read them and discuss their meanings.

exemplify	intuitive	accessible
abrasive	revitalize	visionary
destination	clarify	transplant
display	application	enable

Practice 6: *Complete the following sentences with some of the above key words or phrases. Change the forms if it is necessary.*

1. _____ is an effective way of demonstrating an idea or concept as it provides examples for better understanding.
2. It is important for the presenter to _____ the focus, as well as some key concepts, at the beginning of the presentation.
3. Having the _____ to the Internet is regarded as a must for modern housing.
4. When _____ for a well-paid and respected job, the students need to present a well-written resume and satisfactory skills for actual inter-personal communication.

4.2 Practicing academic vocabulary

Read the following paragraph on "why we need heroes," and focus on the underlined words and phrases. Most of these words and phrases are neither difficult nor new to you, but they are better used in formal or academic settings.

Heroes <u>reveal</u> our missing qualities — Heroes <u>educate</u> us about right and wrong. Most fairytales and children's stories <u>serve this purpose</u>, showing kids the kinds of <u>behaviors</u> that are needed to succeed in life, to better society, and to overcome *hardship*. It is <u>*during our youth*</u> that we most need good, healthy adult role models who <u>*demonstrate*</u> *exemplary behavior. But adults need heroic models* <u>*as well*</u>*. Heroes reveal to us the kinds of qualities we need to be in communion with others.*

(Excerpted from the article with the same title written by S. Allison and G. Goethals)

Give a two-minute speech on ONE reason why we do or do not need heroes. You are strongly advised to use formal words as shown above in your speech.

4.3 Strengthening your skills

Group Work: The X factor for success

Work with three or four students as a group. Read biographic stories on some heroic figures, e.g. Putin, Jobs, Gates, Disney, or anyone who you regard as influential or successful. Discuss with your group members your definition of success as well as the characters or qualities required to be successful. The group leader needs to report on the result of the discussion.

Unit Two
Justice

Identifying Key Ideas in Lectures

Lead-in Questions

1. Why is it important to recognize key ideas (or main points) in a lecture?
2. Why do lectures use examples?

Part I　Significance of Identifying Key Ideas

1.1 Guidance

The purpose of a lecture is probably to stimulate students to do work by themselves. The end result of a course must be to try and make a student autonomous, happy to find things out for themselves, not being given things to accept uncritically.

Learners need to know that's the aim of their course — that they'll become individual and independent learners. So a lecturer will aim to present just part of a topic and stimulate students to want to find out more. Understanding the aim or purpose of a lecture helps you decide where to focus your attention. This is useful because you cannot concentrate on everything at once.

Just like academic written texts, academic lectures normally starts with a main thesis, which is supported with a few sub-thesis or ideas. So, students are suggested to focus on the thesis and supporting ideas in order to draw a general picture of the lecture.

1.2 What comes first, main ideas or details?

The following are two articles with opposing views on gay marriage. Try to gather the main points as soon as possible, then share your answers with your classmates. Those who finish the reading within the shortest time may share their strategies with the class.

Reading Text 1

Gay Marriage "Unnatural"
The Rev. Louis P. Sheldon

1　　In everything which has been written and said about ... homosexual marriage ..., the most fundamental but important point has been overlooked. Marriage is both culturally and physiologically compatible but so-called homosexual marriage is neither culturally nor physiologically possible.

2. Homosexuality is not generational. Without the cooperation of a third party, the homosexual marriage is a dead-end street. In cyber language, the marriage is not programmed properly and there are hardware problems as well.

3. At the core of the effort of homosexuals to justify their behavior is the debate over whether or not homosexuality is some genetic or inherited trait or whether it is a chosen behavior. The activists argue that they are a minority and homosexuality is an immutable characteristic.

4. But no school of medicine, medical journal or professional organization such as the American Psychological Association or the American Psychiatric Association has ever recognized the claim that homosexuality is genetic, hormonal or biological.

5. While homosexuals are few in number, activists claim they represent about 10% of the population. More reliable estimates suggest about 10% of Americans are homosexual. They also are the wealthiest, most educated and most traveled group today. Income for the average homosexual is nearly twice that for the average American. They are the most advantaged group in America.

6. Homosexuality is a behavior-based life-style. No other group of Americans have ever claimed special rights and privileges based only on their choice of sexual behavior. Calling a homosexual relationship a marriage won't make it so. There is no use of rhetoric that can clean it beyond what it is: unnatural and against our country's most basic standards. Every respectable public opinion poll demonstrates that nearly 8 of every 10 Americans do not accept the pretense of "homosexual marriage."

(Excerpted from *Why People Are Rude* by The Rev. Louis P. Sheldon)

Reading Text 2

Equal Treatment Is Real Issue—Not Marriage
USA Today

1   With shouting about "gay marriage" headed for a new sound level ... chances for a widely accepted resolution seem slim. Traditionalists see the issue in private, religious terms, and they're in no mood to compromise. They say marriage, by common definition, involves a man and a woman. And for most people, it's just that. In polls, two-thirds of the public supports the normal marriage.

2   But looking through the lenses of history and law, marriage is far from a private religious matter. There has to be compromise. Not only does the state issue marriage licenses, it gives married couples privileged treatment under law. For example, when one spouse dies, the survivor gets a share of continuing Social Security and other benefits. Joint health and property insurance continues automatically. If there's no will, the law protects the survivor's right to inherit. It's the normal order of things, even for households that may have existed for only the shortest time.

3   But some couples next door—even devoted couples of 20 or 30 years' standing— do not have those rights and cannot get them because of their sex. The U.S. Constitution says every person is entitled to equal protection under law. Some state constitutions go farther, specifically prohibiting sexual discrimination. Ironically, people who oppose gay marriages on religious grounds would have their way of making the gay group hardest living conditions.

4   The state must figure a way to avoid discrimination. The hundreds of employers are now extending workplace benefits to unmarried but committed couples. Offering informal "domestic partner" status may be pointing in the right direction. The need is not necessarily to redefine marriage but to assure equal treatment under the law.

(Excerpted from *USA Today* by The Rev. Louis P. Sheldon)

Unit Two Justice

Part II Distinguishing the Main Idea from the Detail

2.1 Conventions of academic lectures

Academic lectures follow a similar structure of academic articles, though less formal and more interactive. The lecturer may rephrase and repeat what has been presented, raise questions, or elicit debates and discussions. The learners are encouraged to involve actively by asking or answering questions.

In real settings, repetition of the whole lecture is highly unlikely. The learners are therefore advised to spare the energy for major ideas while staying sensitive to interesting details. In other words, if you cannot catch everything, prioritize the main ideas, which normally come before the supportive details.

Tips for listening:
- Never start with details!
- Focus on the main ideas. Although academic lectures may start in different ways such as questions, examples or stories, but they will all be directed to the main theme or general organization of the lecture.
- A lecture is normally focused on ONE theme, which is supported with sub-themes. The theme and sub-themes are the main ideas of a lecture. Recognizing and noting them down allows the listener to follow the thread of the argument or the flow of the lecture.

Practice 1: Creating a general view of the lecture (course audio material 2.2)

*Listen to **Part One** of Michael Sandel's lecture on **Justice**, try to answer the following questions:*

1) What is the theme or the main topic of the lecture?

2) How is Professor Sandel going to deliver or organize this lecture?

3) This part touches on some arguments over health care, same-sex marriage, bonuses and bail out in Wall Street, and the gap between rich and poor. Are these examples highly important for you to answer question 1)?

2.2 Hierarchical organization of a lecture

All essays consist of three major parts: the introduction (beginning), body (middle) and conclusion (ending). The structure is also applicable to paragraphs (see the figure below). The introduction normally starts with brief background information relevant to the topic, and then moves on to the declaration of the speaker's viewpoint on the topic. An effective opening captures the audience's interest and provides a clear topic and purpose of the lecture. It is the part that the audiences see first and determine whether they will continue listening.

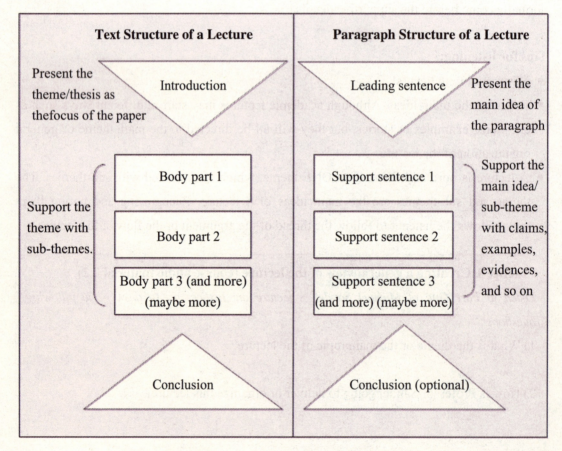

Unit Two　Justice

Practice 2: Finding the thesis "of the lecture" (course audio material 2.2)

*Now, listen to **Part One** of Michael Sandel's lecture on **Justice** again. When you finish listening, try to answer the following questions:*

1) Is this an introductory part of the lecture?

2) Does the speaker introduce the topic of the lecture? When does he do so?

3) In addition to the topic, what else does the speaker introduce in this part?

4) What would you expect to be presented right after this part?

Practice 3: Recognizing place and order of the theme and the supports (course audio material 2.3)

*Now listen to **Part Two** of Michael Sandel's lecture on **Justice**. When you finish, answer the following questions, and share your answer with your classmates.*

1) Is there a focus of this part? What is it?

2) This part consists of four sections. Put them in the correct order according to the original record.

　　a. reasons for answers　　　　　b. central question of the argument
　　c. answers to the question　　　　d. conclusion of the discussion

Tips for speaking:

- Always provide answers before the reasoning.
- Do not include more than one main idea in each paragraph.
- Present the main idea as early as you can.
- Do not include general statements that are not supported with specific details.

2.3 Linking and ending

The body or central part is where the lecturer or speaker explains, clarifies or illustrates the thesis from various perspectives. Each body part focuses on one perspective, hence one sub-theme. While each sub-theme supporting the thesis is supported by specific examples, evidence or statements, there should be natural and logical link between the sub-themes. Appropriate transition makes the smooth flow of the whole speech. The linkage can be either at the end of the previous paragraph, or at the beginning of the following paragraph.

When a detailed explanation has been presented to the audience, a refreshing summarization is necessary. A summary highlights the detailed information and reminds the audience of the main idea once again.

The conclusion is an essential element of writing. It provides an opportunity for the writer to take a fresh look at the writing and make the final justification of the thesis. An academic article can be ended in a variety of ways. In this part, the writer may highlight the main point of the essay, show the awareness and understanding of opposite opinions, offer a recommendation or raise a new series of related questions. When composing an ending, the author should bear in mind that the final impression is by no means less important than the first one, as it is what the reader eventually leaves with.

> **Practice 4: Composing a smooth link and an effective ending (course audio material 2.3)**
> Now listen to **Part Two** of Michael Sandel's lecture on **Justice** again. This time, you should focus on the development of this part. Fill in the following table, and discuss with your partner about how this paragraph is developed and concluded.

Unit Two Justice

Beginning	1. Aristotle's definition of Justice is _____. 2. But the real questions begin when it comes to arguing _____.
Developing	Take the example of distributing flutes. **Question 1:** _____? Answer 1 to question 1: _____. Answer 2 to question 1: _____. Answer 3 to question 1: _____. Aristotle's answer: _____. **Question 2: Here is a harder question that** _____. Answer 1 to question 2: It is for _____ to all. We hear better music. Aristotle's answer to question 2: The essential nature, of musical performance is to _____ . OR Musical performance is not only to _____, but to _____ of the best musicians.
Conclusion	To reason about just distribution of a thing, we have to reason about, _____.OR When we think about justice, we really need to think about the _____ of the activity in question and the qualities that are worth _____.

Tips for closing a lecture or presentation:

- Reinforce the importance of the theme or main idea and bring the paragraph or whole speech to a logical and satisfying closure.
- Reflect on the broader implications of the theme.
- Encourage the audiences to think about the topic in a fresh perspective.

Part III Micro-Skills: Word Families

3.1 Pronunciation practice

Practice the pronunciation of the words in the table and underline the stressed syllable in each word.

Noun	Verb	Adjective
product, production, productivity	produce	productive
analysis	analyze	analytical
economy, economics, economist	economize	economic, economical
popularity	popularize	popular
definition	define	definite, definitive
identification, identity	identify	identified,
introduction	introduce	introductory

3.2 Word formation practice

Practice 5: Changing the meaning by modifying the form (course audio material 2.4)

You can modify the meaning of a word by adding a prefix, e.g., *interpret/misinterpret, assess/reassess, appear/disappear, able/enable/disable.*

Listen to the sentences in the course material, and write in the missing prefix to each word.

1) All trade unions were declared _____ legal by the government.
2) This is one example of a _____ match between the individual's goals and those of the organization.
3) They found no significant _____ relation between class size and levels of achievement.

Unit Two Justice

4) Real estate _____ actions rose by 30 per cent last month.
5) Prices are determined through the _____ action of supply and demand.
6) These animals exhibited _____ normal behavior compared to the control group.

Practice 6: Blank filling (course audio material 2.5)
Listen to the following sentences and complete them with two to five words in each space. Some of the words include prefixes.
1) We had to get _____, because the detail was not very clear on the original ones.
2) Many doctors work _____, which puts them under a lot of stress.
3) Crime prevention is _____ of the police's work, but it is often difficult to assess its effectiveness.
4) Doctors have noticed_____, such as bulimia and anorexia, not just among young women but, surprisingly, among young men.
5) These plants should be grown in partial shade, rather than _____.
6) Researchers have found that _____ are much more likely to be involved in traffic accidents.

Part IV Recycling

4.1 Building your vocabulary

These are the 15 key vocabulary words and phrases for this unit. Read them, discuss their meanings, and try to write down as many words with the same roots as possible.

For example: educational: education, educate, educationist, educated, educative.

majority	essential	fundamental
productive	questionable	call forth
be worthy of	prominent	morality
argument	shed light on	mutual
tendency	intolerance	conviction

Practice 7: *Complete the following sentences with some of the above key words or phrases. Change the forms if it is necessary.*

1. As they must also sprint over short distances, speed is _____.
2. Lying just beneath the surface of those arguments, with passions raging on all sides, are big questions of _____ philosophy, big questions of justice.
3. The government's management capability was once again _____ by the public when another economic crisis took place.
4. The recent government reports _____ the causes of local floods.
5. A great _____ of the staff voted against the new company regulation.

4.2 Practicing sentence patterns

Read the following paragraph and focus on the functional words and phrases that help to cite and comment on others' work and arguments.

*Recognizing and responding to failure are never easy. The Harvard teaching institutions have **developed** a consensus statement for use at the Harvard hospitals that provides a template for helping leaders to respond consistently and ethically to medical errors. Elton John **reminds** us in one of his songs that "sorry" seems to be the hardest word for us to say. Lazare **suggests** that there are cultural perceptions about apologies. He also **proposes** four parts of the process of apology: acknowledgment, remorse, explanation, and offering reparation or reconciliation.*

While speaking, you will sometimes find yourself wanting to cite or comment on other people's research findings. The following expressions may be useful.

based on...(基于)	according to ... (根据)	as suggested by ... (提议)
develop (研发)	propose (提出)	claim (声称)
argue (论证)	question (质疑)	confirm (确认)
hold (保持……观点)	insist (坚持认为)	

Give a two-minute speech reporting the current condition of same-sex marriage in China. Try to support your opinion with research data, official documents, and/or others' statements.

4.3 Strengthening your skills

Group Work: A Survey Report on Students' view on same-sex relationship

Make a survey among your friends and classmates to find out their opinions about gay marriage or same-sex relationship. Report your findings and provide your own argument.

Unit Three
How It's Made

Note-taking

Lead-in Questions

1. Why do students take notes in lectures?
2. How to take lecture notes effectively?

Unit Three   How It's Made

Part I   About Taking Notes in Lectures

1.1 Why do learners take notes in lectures?

Note-taking is the practice of recording information captured from another source. By taking notes, the writer records the essence of the information, freeing their mind from having to recall everything. Effective note-taking from lectures and readings is an essentially surviving skill for university study. Good note-taking allows a permanent record of relevant points that you can integrate with your own speaking and writing, and that can be used for exam revision. The following are some summarizations of reasons for taking notes by learners:

1. *Making yourself take notes forces you to listen carefully and test your understanding of the material.*
2. *When you are reviewing, notes provide a gauge to what is important in the text.*
3. *Personal notes are usually easier to remember than the text.*
4. *The writing down of important points helps you to remember them even before you have studied the material formally.*
5. *You may be tested on the content of the lectures, and thus you need the notes to revise from.*
6. *Taking notes can help you remind yourself of points you feel obscure in lectures, and then work further on the points.*

1.2 What to take in lectures?

In classrooms, the lecturers usually give clues to what is important to take down.

A. Material written on the blackboard

B. Repetition

C. Emphasis

   1. Emphasis can be judged by tone of voice and gesture.

2. Emphasis can be judged by the amount of time the instructor spends on points and the number of examples he or she uses.

D. Word signals (e.g. "There are two points of view on ..."; "The third reason is ..."; "In conclusion ...")

E. Summaries given at the end of class

F. Reviews given at the beginning of class

1.3 Effective ways to take notes

Each student should develop his or her own method of taking notes, but most students find the following suggestions helpful:

A. Make your notes brief.
  1. Never use a sentence where you can use a phrase. Never use a phrase where you can use a word.
  2. Use abbreviations and symbols, but be consistent.

B. Put most notes in your own words. However, the following should be noted exactly:
  1. Formulas
  2. Definitions
  3. Specific facts

C. Use an outline form and/or a numbering system. Indention helps you distinguish major from minor points.

D. If you miss a statement, write key words, skip a few spaces, and get the information later.

E. Don't try to use every space on the page. Leave room for coordinating your notes with the text after the lecture. (You may want to list key terms in the margin or make a summary of the contents of the page.)

F. Date your notes. Perhaps number the pages.

1.4 Linear note or mind map?

Linear note or outlines tend to proceed down a page, using headings and bullets to structure information. A common system consists of headings that use Roman numerals, letters of the alphabet, and Arabic numerals at different levels. A typical structure would be:

Unit Three How It's Made

I. First main topic
  A. Subtopic
    1. Detail
    2. Detail
  B. Subtopic
II. Second main topic
  A Subtopic

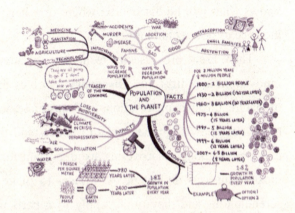

A mind map is a diagram used to visually outline information. A mind map is often created around a single word or text, placed in the center, to which associated ideas, words and concepts are added. Look at the mind map.

Which to choose to take notes in lectures is absolutely determined by learners themselves as both ways are of merits and demerits.

The following is an article on technological advances. Try to take notes while reading, then compare your notes with your classmates to find out some common statements and symbols you share. If you take a linear note, think about whether you could turn it into a mind map.

Reading Text

Technological Advances: Discovery, Invention, Innovation, Diffusion

William Spaulding

1 Technology is the single greatest factor that distinguishes modern economies from primitive ones. Because technology lowers the cost of production and provides new products, it increases both productive and allocative efficiency for all firms. However, technology is unpredictable. No one

knows what will be discovered where or when. Indeed, it is very difficult even to measure the pace of new technology.

2   There are 4 processes to technological advances in an economy: discovery, invention, innovation, and diffusion. **Discovery** involves the elucidation of the fundamental processes of nature through observations of nature, reasoning, and experimentation. Science is the branch of knowledge that seeks to understand the fundamental nature and processes of the universe. Although discoveries are important for providing the fundamentals of knowledge, most businesses do not invest money to make discoveries because discoveries are often serendipitous and they rarely apply to a particular business, which is why a large part of science is financed by the government. Moreover, most governments allow the business to patent the new product or process as an invention.

3   **Invention** is the discovery or development of a product or process by applying previous knowledge in new ways. Inventions often begin as prototypes, in which the essential features are developed to see if they are workable. These prototypes, or basic working models, are then improved by adding, subtracting, or modifying the characteristics of the prototype until no other improvements can be made based on the prototype.

4   To motivate people to invent, governments generally grant patents, which gives the patent holder exclusive rights to sell the patented product or method for a specific period of time. Most patents have a duration of 20 years from the filing of the patent application.

5   **Innovation** is applying basic discoveries or inventions to produce a useful product or process for a specific application. Product innovation is the development of new and improved products or services; process innovation refers to new or improved methods of production or distribution. Innovations cannot be patented, even though often times the distinction between inventions and innovations is blurry.

6   Discoveries and inventions are rarely profitable in themselves. Innovation is necessary to bring the product to market economically.

7   **Diffusion** is the spread of innovation to other firms so that they can remain competitive. This diffusion occurs by either emulating or copying others' products or processes, which is achieved in several ways. First, a company can look at any patents, which are available for inspection by anyone, to see the essential design, and develop new ways of working around that, developing ideas or methods to achieve the same functionality

Unit Three How It's Made

but without infringing the patent. Since patents are narrow in scope, a patent may reveal ways around it, enabling a competitor to develop a process or product that is functionally equivalent to the patented product or process. In other cases, competing firms can reverse engineer the product to see how it works and to see how it could be improved.

(Excerpted from *Technological Advances: Discovery, Invention, Innovation, Diffusion, Research and Development* by William Spaulding)

Part II Notes on a Process

2.1 The facts about process description

A process is essentially any procedure that converts inputs into outputs. A process analysis essay explains a series of events. Often process analysis essays are written chronologically so that readers can perform a set of steps. Similarly, a learner is possible to listen to a lecturer introducing the procedure of an experiment or a manufacturing. Like the writing of a process analysis essay, you need to understand the steps involved in a process, how they relate to one another and how they lead to the end result. Therefore, to take an accurate note on the process helps a learner to review and duplicate the steps by himself.

Tips for listening:

- Understand the general organization of the process analysis.
- Focus on the brief introduction in which a learner can be guided to the materials needed and sometimes a simple generalization of the process.
- Follow the sequence and pay special attention to the semantic markers like first, then, after that, finally, etc. These semantic markers definitely point to the steps of the process, which would be taken notes on.
- It is always a fact that the lecturer or writer would interrupt the process by explaining some special cautions, and once again take notes and underline them.

Practice 1: Understand the pattern of talking about a process (course audio material 3.1).

Now, listen to an excerpt of a report on soap making and take notes.

How to make soap

    Ingredients

  1) _____

    Lye or sodium hydroxide

Oil (different oils are used)
2) _____ makes a harder soap.
3) _____ makes a soap that produces suds.
4) the palm kernel oil
5) _____ makes a soap fragrant (sometimes not included for the case of _____ skin).

Other ingredients for looks and texture
6) _____
7) _____
There are 8) _____ **steps in soap making.**

2.2 Semantic markers

Discourse context and semantic marking are two major factors determining the presence and domain of focus. As an effective way of the later, semantic markers, words and phrases that help signal the progression of ideas in an expression are essential to help a learner precisely receive the information. Semantic markers can perform various functions, such as showing the chronology of events (*firstly, then, after that, next, eventually, in the end*), a cause and effect relationship (*since, because, so, consequently, due to, this explain why ...*), summing up (*in short, to sum up, if I can just sum up*), rephrasing (*in other words, let me put it this way*) and so on. These expressions help a learner to follow and navigate easily through a lecture or a text.

Practice 2: Track the steps with the help of semantic markers. (course audio material 3.1)

Now, listen to the excerpt again and take notes on the steps.

Process of making soap

Step 1: First _____

_____

Step 2: Then _____

_____

Step 3: Then _____

_____

Step 4: Next _____

_____

Step 5: Later _____

_____

Tips for speaking:

When a learner is required to introduce a process in a seminar, the tips below can help structure a complete and coherent oral report.

- Like a process essay, the oral report is organized in an "introduction + body + conclusion" structure.
- In the introductory part, explain materials needed and briefly tell how many steps are included.
- Then follow naturally the chronological order of the procedure. Draw the attention of the audience on the special points if there are any.
- Use the above mentioned semantic markers to help clarify the steps so that the audience can easily follow.
- Explain the output criteria of the procedure, give audience the parameter.

Practice 3: Learn the process—how to make carved candles (course audio material 3.2)

Prediction: *Look at the following pictures and predict the possible flow of how a carved candle is made.*

A _____

B _____

Unit Three How It's Made

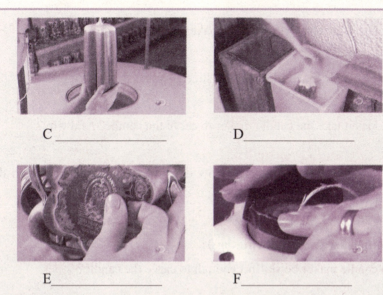

C_____   D_____

E_____   F_____

The possible process:

(   ) → (   ) → (   ) → (   ) → (   ) → (   )

Then watch and listen to the video, and find out the proper verbs to fill in the blanks A—F describing the steps of candle making.

Practice 4: Learn the process—how to make carved candles (course audio material 3.2)

Note-taking: *Watch the video again and answer the questions below.*

Introduction (background)

1. What kind of artifact is carved candles?

Body (the procedure / steps)

2. Why is the candle dipped into cool water?

3. How many times is the candle core dyed with different colors?

45

4. While dipping, what else is the candle maker supposed to do?

5. How does the candle maker do with the sliced "waste"?

6. How long does it take the candle maker to carve the candle? And why?

7. How many rows are totally carved? How does the candle maker do with the second and the last rows?

Digression (other necessary information)

8. How can a candle maker be skillful enough to carve the candle?

9. How can the carving not be ruined when the candle is lit?

Conclusion (completion of the procedure)

10. What is the last step for?

Unit Three   How It's Made

Part III   Micro-Skills: Understanding Sentence Stress

3.1 Reading practice

Read the following sentence and underline the syllables that you think would be stressed. Then listen to this extract, and mark the main stressed syllables in the sentence.

..., that you could always hire a lot of people at low labour rates, but who were in reasonably good health, who were literate and who had reasonable skills.

Note: The speaker chooses to stress words which are particularly important to what he is saying. These tend to be *content words*, rather than function words.

One problem in listening is often that the *unstressed words* tend to be:

- pronounced in unexpected ways, for example, *that* and *were*.
- compressed together, so that it is difficult to hear where one word ends and another begins, for example, *a lot of people*.

3.2 Listen to the sentence stress

Practice 5: Listen to the following sentence. (course audio material 3.3)

The **Japanese** 1) _____ **never** run 2) _____ market **economy. Neither** 3) _____ the **Koreans**.

a) Complete the sentences with one to three words in each blank.
b) The missing words are function words which are unstressed.

- How easy or difficult was it to hear these words?
- If it was difficult, could you work out what they were from the context?

3.3 Read the following extract from a lecture about market research

Note: The lecturer is making the point that when you are collecting market research data through a questionnaire, you need to test out the questionnaire on a small number of people to check that it works well before you carry out the real survey.

Practice 6: Listen to the extract and complete the sentences with two to seven words in each space. (course audio material 3.4)

You need to pre-test the questionnaire. This is really important. Those of you, some of you, will be doing this for your dissertation. Some of you, I know, 1) _____. You need to pro-test the thing, because you're the researcher. You're very 2) _____. You know what you're talking about. But you've got to check that other people do as well. And if you want a statistically valid sample of a hundred people or two hundred people, 3) _____ you're collecting the data properly. And it's here that these 4) _____, they're going to tell you whether it's going to work or not.

So make sure that you do pilots, and, you know, this can be, sort of, 5) _____ different people that you question. I mean, you'll soon find out whether you've got any potential ... or any doubts about the length of the questionnaire, 6) _____, or whether the sort of questions that you're asking are valid. You'll soon find out from that. So piloting or pre-testing is really important.

Look at the words that you wrote in the blanks in the above section and answer the following questions.

a) Which words were stressed?

b) What kind of words were unstressed? How were these words pronounced? Was it difficult to hear them?

Sound advice: Some of the missing words in 3.3 are unstressed and difficult to hear. Because they are function words, you do not usually need to understand them to follow the meaning. Function words are very common words which often show the relationships between ideas in the sentence. So it is important to understand them correctly.

Unit Three   How It's Made

Part IV   Recycling

4.1 Building your vocabulary

These are the 15 key vocabulary words and phrases for this unit. Read them, discuss their meanings.

ingredient	artisan	dissolve	sustainably	pour into
evaporate	elaborate	crucial	shape into	decorate
slice	inventive	combination	wrap	mix with

> **Practice 7:** *Complete the following sentences with some of the above key words or phrases. Change the forms if it is necessary.*
> 1. Exceptional creative or _____ capacity is the product of an inexhaustible willingness to take great trouble.
> 2. A study of Martian geology is _____ toward revealing clues into the history of the Earth.
> 3. One method of reducing heat loss is to _____ the baby in an insulating material.
> 4. Today we are honored having four experts on our show, they will _____ on the topic and share with us their opinions.
> 5. Nature-based tourism would mean less jobs immediately but would be _____.

4.2 Practicing sentence patterns

Read the following paragraph and focus on the function words and phrases that help to explicit the process.

> *After the microwaves pass through the first polarising filter, they are restricted to only vibrating vertically. Before this filter, they could be going towards the filter at any angle/tilt. Then, after the first filter comes, the second filter which comes for now is in the same plane as the first filter. Remember that the first polarising filter has already*

plane polarised in this exact same direction, so they can pass freely through the second filter, to be detected by the receiver.

When explaining a process, you sometimes find it is not enough by just following the steps naturally in a time order. Therefore, to make your explanation logical, you could use some of the following expressions.

| first / second / thirdly | then | next |
| after / before | later | lastly/finally |

Oral Practice: Describe a process of making a simple daily product without naming it. The other students try to figure out what the product is. Use the above function words if possible.

4.3 Strengthening your skills

Group Work: A Research Report on Literature Reading

Read a paper in an authoritative journal of your major or a field you feel interested in, analyze the paper and fill out the following chart. Report in class how the author(s) conducted a research. Try to be detailed on explaining the research method(s).

Title of the Paper	
Author(s) / Affiliation(s)	
Journal/Volume	
Purpose of the Research	

Unit Three How It's Made

Method(s)	
Results	
Conclusions	
Our Comment on the Paper / Research	

Unit Four
Health and Fitness

Active Listening and Digression

Lead-in Questions

1. What are the factors leading to a failure in understanding a lecturer?
2. How can a learner listen actively?
3. Why does a lecturer sometimes digress?

Unit Four   Health and Fitness

Part I   Listen Actively

1.1 What impairs listening?

"Active listening" means, as its name suggests, fully concentrating on what is being said rather than just "hearing" the message of the speaker. Active listening involves listening with all senses. Active listening intentionally focuses on who you are listening to, in order to understand what he or she is saying. As a learner, you should then be able to repeat back in your own words what they have said to their satisfaction. This does not mean you are interested in what he or she has said or agree with the person, but rather you understand what they have said.

What do you think of the subject matter? Have you got a lot of experience with it? Will it be hard to understand, or simple?	Is the lecturer experienced or nervous? What are his/her non-verbal cues? What is his/her frame of mind?
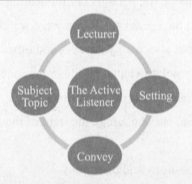	
Is the message illustrated with visual support? Is technology used effectively? Are unfamiliar terms properly defined, or illustrated with examples?	Is the space conducive to listening, or to interaction or exchange with the lecturer? Are there avoidable distractions?

1.2 How to listen actively?

Prepare with a positive, engaged attitude

1. Focus your attention on the subject

   Stop all non-relevant activities beforehand to orient yourself to the speaker or the topic

2. Review mentally what you already know about the subject

   Organize in advance relevant material in order to develop it further (previous lectures, TV programs, newspaper articles, web sites, prior real life experience, etc.)

3. Avoid distractions:

   Seat yourself appropriately close to the speaker

   Avoid distractions (a window, a talkative neighbor, noise, etc.)

4. Acknowledge any emotional state

   Suspend emotions until later, or

   Passively participate unless you can control your emotions

5. Set aside your prejudices, your opinions

   You are present to learn what the speaker has to say, not the other way around.

Actively listen

1. Be other-directed; focus on the person communicating

   Follow and understand the speaker as if you were walking in their shoes

   Listen with your ears but also with your eyes and other senses

2. Be aware: non-verbally acknowledge points in the speech

   Let the argument or presentation run its course

   Don't agree or disagree, but encourage the train of thought

3. Be involved:

   Actively respond to questions and directions

   Use your body position (e.g. lean forward) and attention to encourage the speaker and signal your interest

The following life-expectancy quiz is one of many health questionnaires now used by doctors, medical centers and insurance groups. While quizzes can hardly be precise, they do give a more realistic picture of probable longevity than old-fashioned actuarial tables which relied almost exclusively on the subject's heredity patterns and medical history. Finish the

Unit Four   Health and Fitness

quiz and find out how long you will live, and then work in groups to map the factors contributing to longevity.

Live-expectancy Quiz

How Long Will You Live

Start with the number 72.

Personal facts:

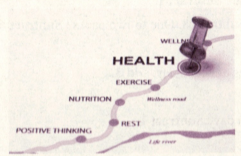

If you are male, **subtract 3**.

If female, **add 4**.

If you live in an urban area with a population over 2 million, **subtract 2**.

If you live in a town under 10,000 or on a farm, **add 2**.

If any grandparent lived to 85, **add 2**.

If all four grandparents lived to 80, **add 6**.

If either parent died of a stroke or heart attack before the age of 50, **subtract 4**.

If any parent, brother or sister under 50 has (or had) cancer or a heart condition, or has had diabetes since childhood, **subtract 3**.

Do you earn over ¥200,000 a year? **Subtract 2**.

If you finished college, **add 1**. If you have a graduate or professional degree, **add 2 more**.

If you are 65 or over and still working, **add 3**.

If you live with a spouse or friend, **add 5**. If not, **subtract 1** for every ten years alone since age 25.

Running Total

Life-style status:

If you work behind a desk, **subtract 3**.

If your work requires regular, heavy physical labor, **add 3**.

If you exercise strenuously (tennis, running, swimming, etc.) five times a week for at least a half-hour, **add 4**. Two to three times a week, **add 2**.

Do you sleep more than ten hours each night? **Subtract 4**.

Are you intense, aggressive, easily angered? **Subtract 3**.

Are you easygoing and relaxed? **Add 3**.

Are you happy? **Add 1**. Unhappy? **Subtract 2**.

Have you had a speeding ticket in the past year? **Subtract 1**.

Do you smoke more than two packs a day? **Subtract 8**. One to two packs? **Subtract 6**. One-half to one? **Subtract 3**.

If you drink half a liter of wine, or four glasses of beer a day, **add 3**.

If you don't drink alcohol every day, **add 1**.

Do you drink the equivalent of 43g of liquor a day? **Subtract 1**.

If you are a heavy drinker, **subtract 8**.

Are you overweight by 23kg or more? **Subtract 8**. By 14 to 23kg? **Subtract 4**. By 4.5 to 14 kg? **Subtract 2**.

If you are a man over 40 and have annual checkups, **add 2**.

If you are a woman and see a gynaecologist (妇产科医生) once a year, **add 2**.

Running Total

Age adjustment:

If you are between 30 and 40, **add 2**.

If you are between 40 and 50, **add 3**.

If you are between 50 and 70, **add 4**.

If you are over 70, **add 5**.

Add up your score to get your life expectancy.

(Modified from the book *Lifegain,* by Robert F. Allen, Ph D., Appleton Books Inc. TIME, NOVEMBER 2, 1991)

Unit Four Health and Fitness

Part II Digression

2.1 Why does a lecturer digress?

Sometimes a lecturer moves away from the main topic for a while before getting back to it even if he organizes his information well, explicitly. This is defined as digression in lectures. There might be the following reasons for a lecturer to digress during his lecture:

1. to define a new term or jargon
2. to give reference to a book or a citation on the topic
3. to comment on the point he is making
4. to talk about the organizing of the lecture
5. to give a personal anecdote to illustrate a point

Tips for listening:
- identify that there is a digression
- decide whether it is important to take notes or not
- make sure that the lecturer is back to the main topic

> **Practice 1: Listen to the extract, then read the script, and underline the digression(s). Discuss with your partner why the lecturer digresses. (course audio material 4.1)**
>
> My first set of examples come from a — and I'm going to talk about some fairly classic experiments in this lecture, but I would point out before I go on that there is a really excellent chapter on this subject in Shettleworth's book, which is referred to in the reference list for this lecture. Sara Shettleworth has a superb chapter on social learning. It's called "Learning from Others." It's very up-to-date, very thoughtful, very comprehensive, and I'm just going to mention just a few of the examples that she mentions. But if you seriously want to think about this area, and it involves many complexities, her chapter is a very good place to go. Anyway, some of the best-known work on social learning, or putative social learning, in rats, in animals, are about food preferences. These are

examples of learning the significance of stimuli, learning what foods are good to eat and what foods are bad to eat.

2.2 How to detect a digression?

In a lecture, the lecturer would always remind the audience of the transient distraction from the main topic by using semantic markers when he begins and finishes doing it. The semantic markers include:

By the way, ...
I might note in passing ...
Before I go on ...
Although it is not strictly speaking relevant to our topic, perhaps I might say something about ...
... good place to go

Practice 2: Listen to a lecture about how to design questionnaires. In this part, the lecturer is talking about general design issues in preparing questionnaires. (course audio material 4.2)

Listen, take notes on the main ideas of the lecture, label the digression and decide whether you need to take notes on the digression.

1. Main ideas:

2. Is there any digression? Is it important? What is it about?

3. Compare your notes with your partner. Did you miss any ideas in your notes?

4. How does the lecturer begin and end the digression?

Unit Four Health and Fitness

Tips for speaking:

As a learner, you also need to digress from time to time to give further information to your audience in a presentation. To do this, you are explaining, illustrating, even arousing interests from your audience.

- Use the semantic markers to remind the audience that there is a digression
- Explain the reasons for digression
- Only detach from the main topic to arouse the audience's interests

Practice 3: You are going to watch a talk from Graham Hill on vegetarianism. In this video, he is elaborating on reasons for taking a vegetarian diet. (course audio material 4.3)

Leading-in Activity: Group Discussion

- Are you a vegetarian? Why or why not?
- Do you think vegetarianism would be a prevailing life style? Why or why not?

Listening Activity: Note-taking

Listen to the talk and fill in the following blanks.

The digression in his speech is: 1. _____

(The purpose of digression: 2. _____)

The main idea of his speech: 3. _____
_____

Listen to the talk again and take notes on the details.

The reasons for the speaker to be a vegetarian:

4. _____
5. _____
6. _____

The reason that he was hesitating:

7. _____
_____

A third solution:

8. _____

The benefits:

9. _____
10. _____
11. _____
12. _____

Ending of the talk:

13. _____

Practice 4: Talk about health (course audio material 4.4)

Watch the video, and think about the following questions.

Are there any digressions in the talk? Are they important? Is it necessary for learners to take notes on them? Why or why not?

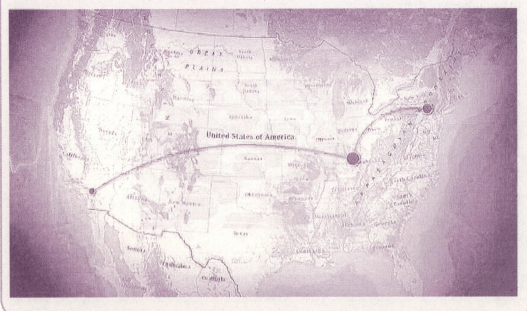

Unit Four Health and Fitness

Watch the video again and take notes.

The elements in the formula for life and good health:

1. _____ 2. _____ 3. _____

The speaker's experiences of living in different places in the U.S.:

4. Fill in the chart:

Places			
Years staying there			
Condition of his lungs			
Environmental problems			

The problem with medical treatment:

5. _____

_____

61

Part III　Micro-Skills: General Academic Words in Lectures

When a learner learns English as a second language, he is usually taught the standard variant of the language. This involves mostly written English and its uses, but not always spoken English. Whether the difference between written and spoken English is in one sense vast or in other senses unimportant all depends on how the language is intended to be used. In the case of academic English classroom, the learner can overcome the gap by preparing himself with what the lecturer would talk about in a lecture.

Actually, in a lecture, a lecturer would use many general academic words or phrases to talk about his views and ideas in his field of study. Learn these words and phrases can help the learner better concentrate on the specific information he might listen to in the class.

3.1 Reading practice

Read the following excerpt of studies on American sedentary lifestyles. Underline main ideas, keywords and function words.

Americans are more sedentary than ever, government surveys show. That is a problem even among people who exercise regularly.

A study that followed more than 240,000 adults over 8½ years found that watching a large amount of television was associated with a higher risk of death, including cardiovascular disease, even for participants who reported seven or more hours a week of moderate-to-vigorous exercise. The research, published in 2012 in the *American Journal of Clinical Nutrition*, used TV viewing and overall sitting time as a proxy for sedentary behavior.

"Our results suggest that exercise alone may not be enough to eliminate risks associated with too much sitting," says Charles Matthews, lead author of the study and an investigator with the National Institutes of Health. He says estimates from government surveys

Unit Four Health and Fitness

indicate that people's sedentary time outside of work has increased by about 40% between 1965 and 2009.

People who live in Colorado, where obesity rates are relatively low, take an average of 6,500 steps a day, a 2005 study found. By contrast, residents of Tennessee and Arkansas, where the obesity rates are much higher, take an average of 4,500 steps a day. "We don't know that it's cause and effect obviously, but the states with lower obesity rates have the higher number of steps," says James Hill, executive director of the Anschutz Health and Wellness Center at the University of Colorado.

Health experts say people still need moderate to vigorous exercise, which has been shown to reduce risks of cardiovascular disease and other disorders. Dr. Bassett says a doctoral student in his department conducted a study in which 58 people watching 90 minutes of television marched in place in front of the TV during commercial breaks. "They increased their steps by about 3,000 per day just by doing this during commercials," says Dr. Bassett. "That's equivalent to about 30 minutes of walking." The study was published last year in the *International Journal of Behavioral Nutrition and Physical Activity*.

(by Sumathi Reddy, excerpted from March 12, 2013, the U.S. edition of *The Wall Street Journal,* with the headline: Hard Math: Adding Up Just How Little We Actually Move)

3.2 Listening practice

Then listen to a report on a similar topic, pay attention to the different expressions of an idea in writing and speaking.

Practice 5: Listen to the report and fill in the following chart. (course audio material 4.5)

		In the reading passage	In the listening passage
Different expressions		sedentary lifestyle	
		cardiovascular disease and other disorders	
		moderate-to-vigorous exercise	
Similar expressions			
Shared opinions			

Sound advice: From the above practices, learners could see the differences as well as similarities between written and spoken passages. To learn the general academic words is essential for understanding both a writer and a lecturer in an academic communication.

Unit Four Health and Fitness

Part IV Recycling

4.1 Building your vocabulary

These are the 15 key vocabulary words and phrases for this unit. Read them, discuss their meanings.

refer	complexity	appraise	preference	assessment
get out of hand	in conflict with	emission	give ... a shot	in the dark
variety	concentrate	dose	available	lessen

Practice 6: *Complete the following sentences with some of the above key words or phrases. Change the forms if it is necessary.*

1. By the end of the next decade, a simple blood test could alert doctors to a wide _____ of cancer precursors.
2. While intelligent people can often simplify the _____, a fool is more likely to complicate the simple.
3. Because of the rapid development of the Internet industry in China, an abundance of jobs are _____.
4. The authorities couldn't even begin to _____ the damage of the recent landslide in the region, because it was so great.
5. The statement of the male witness was _____ the other evidences, therefore the jurors did not reach a consensus.

65

4.2 Practicing sentence patterns

Read the following paragraph and focus on the function words and phrases that help to describe the graphs.

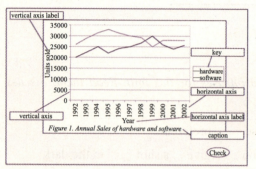

*The graph **shows** the sales figures for two products from 1992 to 2002. The **horizontal** axis represents years and the **vertical** axis represents units of sales. The graph **presents** both the **increase** and **decline** in sales for both products, as sales **fluctuated** during the ten-year period.*

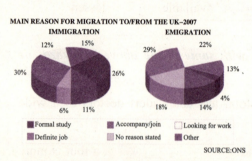

*The pie charts **illustrate** the primary reasons that people came to and left the UK in 2007. At first glance it is clear that the main factor influencing this decision was employment. Having a definite job **accounted for 30 per cent** of immigration to the UK, and this figure was very **similar** for emigration, at 29%. A large number of people, 22%, also emigrated because they were looking for a job, though the **proportion** of people entering the UK for this purpose was **noticeably lower at less than** a fifth.*

*Another major factor influencing a move to the UK was for formal study, with **over a quarter of** people immigrating for this reason. However, only **a small minority**, 4%, left for this.*

*The proportions of those moving to join a family member were quite similar for immigration and emigration, at 15% and 13% respectively. Although **a significant number of** people (32%) gave "other" reasons or did not give a reason why they emigrated, this accounted for only 17% with regards to immigration.*

It is a quite frequent scenario for a learner to listen to an explanation of data collected in a scientific research. He or she may sometimes feels dazzled when hearing the figures and seeing the lines, bars and pies, not to mention he or she is required to give a presentation on his or her research findings. In either of the above cases of listening or speaking, a learner would perform better by learning the following function words.

rise	increase	go up	grow	surge	decrease
fall	drop	decline	plunge	plummet	stay the same
remain constant		level off	stabilize	fluctuate	zigzag
flutter	undulate	bottom out	reach a low/high		peak at
slightly	gently	steadily	gradually	similarly	suddenly
sharply	dramatically	steeply	significantly	a lot	respectively
illustrate	show	present	account for	figure	number
percentage	proportion	rate	ratio		

Oral practice: Draw a pie or bar chart according to the information in the following picture, and then report in class.

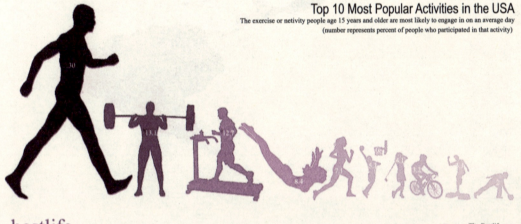

4.3 Strengthening your skills

Group Work: A Survey Report on Healthy Living Habits

Design a questionnaire on learning the living habits of your fellow students, and survey at least 30 students with your questionnaire. Collect the data, analyze your findings and draw a conclusion. Report in class your survey with visual support.

Unit Five
Globalization

How to Introduce New Terminology

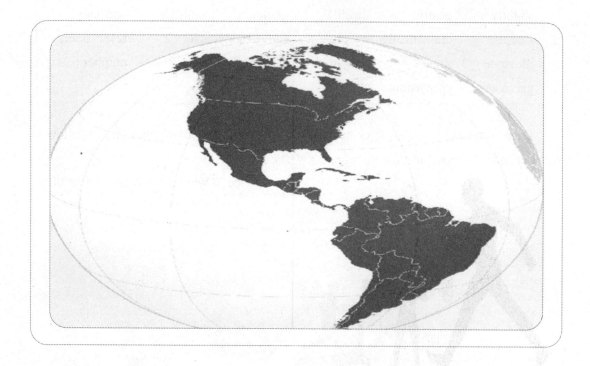

Lead-in Questions

1. Why do lecturers introduce new terminologies in their lectures?
2. How to identify new terminologies as a listener?

Unit Five Globalization

Part I Introduction of New Terminologies

1.1 Why do lecturers introduce new terminologies in their lectures?

A lecturer is a person who is well versed in either specific or multiple subjects, and imparts his advice to an audience in search of knowledge or inspiration. Most commonly, such speakers are experts in their field.

A lecturer always intends to present information or teach people about a particular subject. Lectures are used to convey critical information, history, background, theories and equations. Lecturers usually introduce new terminology to their students during their lectures thus to convey new knowledge to the students. The terms they introduce often represent new and quite abstract concepts which can be difficult to grasp, therefore, how to identify new terminologies, and thoroughly understand them is crucial for the students.

1.2 What do lecturers do to introduce new terminology?

In classrooms, the lecturers usually do the following to help their students understand new terms or concepts.

A. give definitions;

B. provide a number of extended examples;

C. explain how the term or concept works;

D. contrast the new concept with a concept that is already familiar to the students.

Reading Text

Globalization: Don't Worry, Be Happy

1   Nowadays, we hear a lot about the growing threat of globalization, accompanied by those warnings that rich patterns of local life are being undermined, and many dialects and

traditions are becoming extinct. But stop and think for a moment about the many positive aspects that globalization is bringing. Read on and you are bound to feel comforted, ready to face the global future, which is surely inevitable now.

2 Consider the Internet, that prime example of our shrinking world. Leaving aside the all-too-familiar worries about pornography and political extremism, even the most narrow-minded must admit that the net offers immeasurable benefits, not just in terms of education, the sector for which it was originally designed, but more importantly on a global level, the spread of news and comment. It will be increasingly difficult for politicians to maintain their regimes of misinformation, as the oppressed will not only find support and comfort, but also be able to organize themselves more effectively.

3 MTV is another global provider that is often criticized for imposing popular culture on the unsuspecting millions around the world. Yet the viewers' judgment on MTV is undoubtedly positive; it is regarded as indispensable by most of the global teenage generation who watch it, a vital part of growing up. And in the final analysis, what harm can a few songs and videos cause?

4 Is the world dominance of brands like Nike and Coca-cola so bad for us, when all is said and done? Sportswear and soft drinks are harmless products when compared to the many other things that have been globally available for a longer period of time—heroin and cocaine, for example. In any case, just because Nike shoes and Coke cans are for sale, it doesn't mean you have to buy them—even globalization cannot deprive the individual of his free will.

5 Critics of globalization can stop issuing their doom and gloom statements. Life goes on, and has more to offer for many citizens of the world than it did for their parents' generation.

(Retrieved at http://www.manfen5.com/stinfo/)

Unit Five Globalization

Part II Recognizing Signals of Definition

2.1 How can students recognize lecture language that signals a definition?

Lecturers often use new words as they explain new information or ideas. They also use a variety of expressions to present definitions for those words. A quick recognition of those new words and their meanings helps students better understand the lecture.

Here are some signals words and expressions which help students quickly figure out new terms and concepts, thus be more concentrated on them and better understand them.

A. that is ...
B. in other words, ...
C. X, or _____
D. X, meaning _____
E. By X, I mean _____
F. X is the term for _____
G. X means _____
H. What I mean by X is _____
I. What I mean when I say X is _____

Another common signal for a definition is a rhetorical question. Rhetorical questions are given for the purpose of preparing the students for the answer. They are not questions for students to answer, instead, the lecturers themselves offer the answer.

A. What do I mean by X? Well, I mean _____
B. What is X? X is _____

Tips for listening:
- Identify new terms and concepts introduced and write them down immediately.
- Focus on how lecturers introduce the new terms and concepts by identifying the signals.

71

- Further develop your understanding of information centered on the new terms and concepts, make sure whether the lecturers use extended examples, explain how they work or contrast them with those you are familiar with.

Practice 1: Understand how different new terms and concepts are introduced. (course audio material 5.1.1—5.1.5)

Now, listen to a number of excerpts from lectures. As you listen, first write down the term or concept, and then write down the lecture language that signals a definition. Then listen once more and write down the definition.

1. Term: <u>intelligence</u>
   Lecture language: _____
   Definition: _____

2. Term: <u>the DMZ</u>
   Lecture language: _____
   Definition: _____

3. Term: <u>book smart</u>
   Lecture language: _____
   Definition: _____

4. Term: <u>the East End of London</u>
   Lecture language: _____
   Definition: _____

5. Term: <u>free rider problem</u>
   Lecture language: _____
   Definition: _____

2.2 Structural understanding of a lecture with the assistance of mind maps

A mind map is a graphical way to represent ideas and concepts. It is a visual thinking tool that helps structuring information, helping you to better analyze, comprehend, synthesize, recall and generate new ideas.

Unit Five Globalization

In a mind map, as opposed to traditional note taking or a linear text, information is structured in a way that resembles much more closely how your brain actually works. Since it is an activity that is both analytical and artistic, it engages your brain in a much, much richer way, helping in all its cognitive functions. And, best of all, it is fun!

But what can we use mind maps for?

- Note taking
- Brainstorming (individually or in groups)
- Problem solving
- Studying and memorization
- Planning
- Researching and consolidating information from multiple sources
- Presenting information
- Gaining insight on complex subjects
- Jogging your creativity

Mind maps can help clarify your thinking in almost anything, in many different contexts: personal, family, educational or business. Planning your day or planning your life, summarizing a book, launching a project, planning and creating presentations, writing blog posts — well, you get the idea — anything, really.

Practice 2: Understand what globalization is by referring to the mind map (course audio material 5.2)

Briefly study the structure of the lecture according to the mind map.

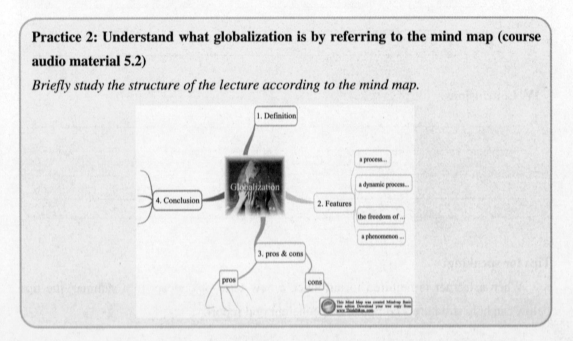

Now, listen to the lecture and complete the exercise based on the above mind map.

I. The Definition of Globalization:
Lecture Language: _____
Definition: _____
_____
_____

II. Features of Globalization: (Note down the key information for each feature.)

1. A process: _____
2. A dynamic process: _____
3. The freedom: _____
4. A phenomenon: _____

III. Pros & Cons of Globalization

Pros: 1. _____
 2. _____
 3. _____
 4. _____
Cons: 1. _____
 2. _____

IV. Conclusions

1. _____
2. _____
3. _____
4. _____

Tips for speaking:

When a learner is required to introduce a new term or concept in a seminar, the tips below can help structure a complete and coherent oral report.

Unit Five Globalization

- First and foremost, give a clear definition of the new term or concept.
- Give further examples if necessary to explain its features or characteristics.
- Sometimes it's rather necessary to compare its advantages and disadvantages.
- Draw your conclusion in accordance with the definition thus to make your oral report coherent.

Practice 3: Globalization (course audio material 5.3)

I. Warm-up: Based on what you've read and listened to in Practice 5.2, predict in what aspects of life globalization exists. Compare your prediction with that of your classmates.

A _____
B _____
C _____
D _____

II. Watch the video and answer the following questions.

1. What is the most outstanding characteristic of globalization?

2. In which areas of life does globalization exist?

3. What does it mean that technology of communication and mass media are global standard?

4. How can NGOs influence the process of globalization?

5. In which way do small sites suffer from political globalization?

6. What does the term "Networld" mean?

7. How can countries like China and India benefit from globalization?

8. Why do most sub-Saharan countries suffer from globalization?

9. Why is globalization both threat and opportunity to industrialized countries?

10. Dictation of the ending.

   Do a dictation of the ending of the lecture starting with "It becomes clear that ..." and understand how the ending echoes the introduction.

Part III Micro-Skills: Weak Forms of Function Words

3.1 Read and think

Look at the sentence below and then answer the questions that follow.

There are a number of different ways that a lecturer can make new concepts easier for students to understand.

1) How many function words can you identify in the sentence above that would probably be unstressed in normal speech?

2) Write five more function words in your notebook.

3) Why is it useful to be aware of unstressed function words when you are listening to lectures?

3.2 Reading practice

Read the following pairs of sentences. What is the difference in the pronunciation of the bold words in each pair? What might explain this difference?

1. What time **does** the train leave?

   I'm not sure why he's late. He **does** know about the meeting.

2. **Some** researchers have taken a different approach.

   We've just got time for **some** questions.

3. I'm not sure what you're getting **at**.

   There were **at** least five errors in the program.

4. Increasingly, small memory devices **can** store large amounts of data.

   Well, I **can** do it, but I don't want to.

5. Oh, are they going to interview **us** as well as the students?

   Can you tell **us** what you've found?

6. It was heated to 150 ℃ **for** 10 minutes.

   There are arguments **for** and against GM crop trials.

Note: Normally these words in bold are unstressed. In oral English utterances, many function words, such as conjunctions, articles, prepositions and auxiliary verbs, are difficult to hear when they are unstressed.

3.3 Listen to understand weak forms of function words in English.

Practice 4: Listen and complete the extract with three to five words in each space. In each case, at least one of the missing words is a function word. (course audio material 5.4)

Multiple-choice questions—dead easy. They reduce interviewer bias; very easy for people to ... very easy and fast for people to answer; very 1) _____.
But the argument goes that they are rather difficult to design. The thing about multiple-choice questions is that 2) _____ into certain answers. This is a good 3) _____. If you have a multiple-choice question and you pilot it, you may find that people are not, they don't put the issue that you're asking them into that particular 4) _____ that you've imposed. So that's where 5) _____ will help. Let me just show you an example of this.

78

Unit Five Globalization

Part IV Recycling

4.1 Building your vocabulary

These are the 15 key vocabulary words and phrases for this unit. Read them, discuss their meanings.

globalization	interconnected	indispensable	advancement	mobility
instantaneous	substantial	multinational	exert	diversity
undermine	shrink	in terms of	tend to	eat up

Practice 5: *Complete the following sentences with some of the above key words or phrases. Change the forms if it is necessary.*

1. Globalization sharply increases competition worldwide, thus small companies are more likely to _____ by big companies.
2. The most outstanding feature of globalization is the _____ between individuals and nations.
3. An undeniable trend of globalization is that the world _____ and is becoming a global village.
4. Critics blame that globalization _____ dialects, local customs and cultural diversity.
5. Globalization exerts influence in almost every aspect of our life _____ economy, politics and culture.

4.2 Practicing sentence patterns

Read the following paragraph and focus on the lecture language that helps to define and introduce new terminology.

   One pretty common distraction display was called the broken wing display. And in a broken wing display the bird spreads and drags the wings or its tail, and while it does that, it slowly moves away from the nests so it really looks like a bird with a broken wing. And these broken wing displays can be pretty convincing.

When introducing a new terminology, you'd better first and foremost define what it is. Then unfold the new terminology by either explaining its features, how it works or exemplifying it. Therefore, a logical and coherent development is crucial to the arrangement of your information.

Oral practice: Introduce the one-child policy of China to your partner. Try to follow the outline below:

Topic: The One-child Policy of China

Introduction: What is the one-child policy

Further development: 1. Review the history of the one-child policy
　　　　　　　　　　　2. Discuss its advantages and disadvantages

Future: Predict the future trend of the policy

4.3 Strengthening your skills

Project-based Task: A Research Report on the Science of Global Warming

Work in groups of 5 members, make a research on Global Warming based on the following mind map, and then give your presentation in class. Provide PPT or visual assistance of videos if necessary.

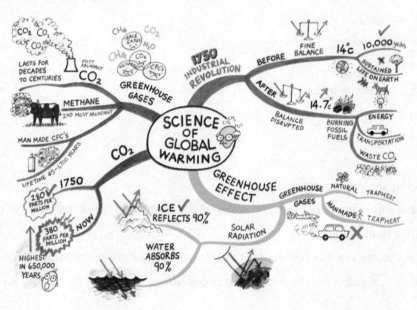

Unit Six
Let's Put Birth Control Back on the Agenda

What Lecturers Do in Lectures

Lead-in Questions

1. What do lecturers usually include in their lectures?
2. How may lecturers arrange information in their lectures?

Part I What Lecturers Do in Lectures?

1.1 Who is a lecturer?

A lecturer is a person who is well versed in either specific or multiple subjects, and imparts his advice to an audience in search of knowledge or inspiration. Most commonly, such speakers are experts in their field. However, as can be testified by anyone who has ever sat through a boring lecture, not all of these orators are trained in public speaking.

On the professional lecture circuit, you can find a host of celebrities, politicians, and authors. The purpose of their lectures can come in many forms. Some take the podium to promote a personal cause, while others may be relating life experiences for the entertainment of the crowd. Some lecturers are attempting to make a persuasive argument, convincing those who listen that their views or opinions are more correct than those of others. Some are simply promoting a book, movie, or product, interspersing amusing anecdotes amidst the sales pitch.

1.2 What do lecturers do in a lecture?

Writers use different structures to organize their writing. For example, they might use this structure.

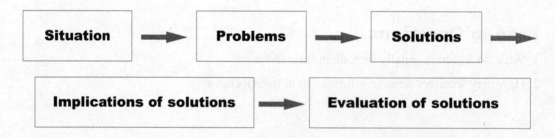

In a similar way, lecturers may also use different structures to organize their lectures. Here are some examples of what lecturers might do during a lecture.

Unit Six   Let's Put Birth Control Back on the Agenda

Lecture Structure 1

Suggest alternative methods of doing something
↓
Discuss the benefits and drawbacks of each method

Lecture Structure 2

State a hypothesis
↓
Outline an experiment to test the hypothesis
↓
Look at the results of the experiment
↓
Draw conclusions from the results

Lecture Structure 3

Present a theory
↓
See how the theory works in practice
↓
Suggest problems with the theory

1.3 Sound advice

Recognizing the structure of a lecture may help you understand the main ideas that the lecturer is trying to communicate. As you listen to a lecture, ask yourself:

• What is the lecturer doing at this point in the lecture?

• How does this part of the lecture relate to the other parts of the lecture?

These questions will help you get the "big-picture"—i.e., the main ideas—of the lecturer's argument.

1.4 Questions for discussion

Think of the lectures you have listened to. In groups, discuss the following questions.

• Can you think of any lectures where the lecturers used these structures?

• Can you think of any other ways in which lecturers organize their lectures?

Reading Text

Birth Control for Men? For Real This Time?

Jessica Mack

1 When the birth control pill hit the U.S. market 51 years ago, the hope had been for a male method to follow close at its heels. Yet, despite decades of research and periodic hopeful headlines, progress has been largely indiscernible.

2 Now, researchers are touting new developments: a reversible vasectomy, a "dry orgasm" pill and a miracle plant from Indonesia, to name a few. The

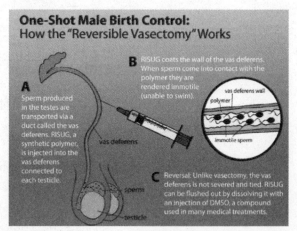

demand appears to be there, considering that 1 in 6 U.S. men over age 35 has had a vasectomy. But with so many false alarms, should we believe that this time's the charm?

Unit Six Let's Put Birth Control Back on the Agenda

3   Research on male contraception began in the 1970s, initially focusing on the use of hormones to manipulate sperm production. But while trials demonstrated efficacy, results were marred by nasty side effects and onerous administration (one potential method combined an implant below the skin with monthly injections).

4   A decade later, Elaine Lissner was just graduating college with a big idea: She founded the Male Contraception Information Project (MCIP) in the late 1980s to track progress and raise awareness of male contraception. Lissner says, "I thought everything would change quite quickly, [but] the world wasn't ready ... for male contraception in 1992. Everyone was focused on HIV and [the abortion pill], and nobody had time for [this]. I couldn't get any funding."

5   "Only nonprofits and universities continued to work [on this]," says Regine Sitruk-Ware, executive director for research and development at Population Council and a veteran researcher in the field. Then, in 2003, the mapping of the human genome enabled a change in gears. Instead of tampering with the body's hormones overall, researchers could zero in on specific mechanisms to affect sperm viability. Now research is focused mainly on nonhormonal methods, as well as those with added benefits such as protection from HIV or baldness.

6   One such method, likely to be the first on the market, is RISUG, or the "reversible vasectomy." Currently in Phase III trials in India, it entails a one-time injection into the vas deferens of a harmless chemical solution that deactivates sperm passing through it from the testes to the penis. So far RISUG has proven to be effective, safe—and reversible with a second injection.

7   Several other methods are just around the corner. Plant-based pills, like one being manufactured from the gandarusa plant in Indonesia, may offer natural, nonhormonal options. Researchers in the U.K. are working on a "dry orgasm" pill based on medications that restrict sperm from becoming semen—thus orgasm occurs but ejaculation does not. Other methods, such as the use of moderate heat or ultrasound on the testicles, are noninvasive and relatively simple ways of inhibiting sperm production.

8   But obstacles still loom. Contraception is about many things—reproductive choice, personal freedom, partner trust—but perhaps mostly about money. In 2015, the global contraceptives market for men and women will reach an estimated $17.2 billion, yet industry players have

done little to sustain male-method development (beyond or even including male condoms) because they still don't see potential demand or dollars.

9   "Market research has shown little interest from males, so companies have continued to [bow] out," says Sitruk-Ware. The problem with such research is that it's based on a premise that could change once an actual product is available. That was the case with the vaginal-ring contraceptive NuvaRing: Initial projections said women would be uninterested. Yet recent NuvaRing sales in the U.S. are up more than 40 percent.

10   Luckily, the odyssey for a male method is benefiting from recent broad momentum around contraception globally. "The difference now is that we've been through a lot of years of consciousness raising," says Lissner. "There's a reason I stuck this out."

(Excerpted from the Fall 2011 issue of Ms.)

Unit Six Let's Put Birth Control Back on the Agenda

Part II Structure Analysis of a Lecture

2.1 The Top-Down strategy in listening

Top-Down strategy in listening focuses on the meaning of the text that the learners listen. It gives attention for the gist of the listening text rather than for each and individual components. The learners are expected to give the meaning of the text they listen based on their background knowledge.

Top-Down helps the learners to understand the listening text without worrying about the smaller components of the language. From its nature this strategy is said to be an "automatic method" because it automatically focuses on the meaning. The learners are expecting to comprehend the main idea of the listening activities based on their prior knowledge. In addition, it helps the learners guess unfamiliar words or phrases contextually.

Also, Top-Down enhances prediction abilities of the learners. In order to comprehend text background knowledge has its own effect. The learners evolve their language by predicting the gist of the text if and only if they have background knowledge. The skills they have used to understand the text are vital for their language acquisition because when they implement this strategy, they also develop their guessing ability of the whole message.

Tips for listening:
- Make prediction about the lecture based on the topic given;
- During listening, focus on the brief introduction to quickly narrow down the topic and fit your prediction into your listening;
- Grasp signals that indicate the structural development of the lecture;
- Pay attention to the collusion and figure out how coherent it is to the introduction.

Practice 1: Understand China's one-child policy. (course audio material 6.1)

Briefly study the mind-map on China's One-child Policy before listening to the report.

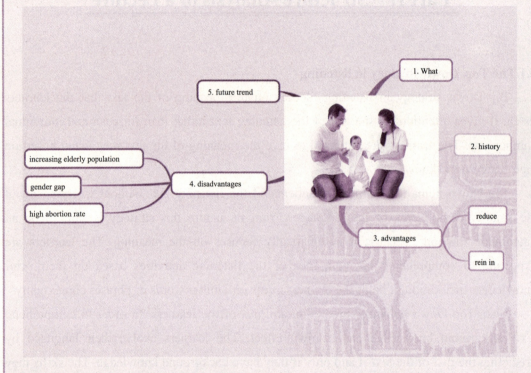

Now, listen to an excerpt of the report on China's One-child Policy.

I. Structure of the report

1. **What**

    A regulation under which each couple is allowed to _____.

2. **History**

    It has been introduced in China _____.

3. **Advantages**

    1) Reduce _____;

    2) Rein in _____.

4. **Disadvantages**

    1) The elderly population quickly _____ while the young labor force will start to _____.

    2) _____ because of a traditional culture that favors boys more than girls.

Unit Six Let's Put Birth Control Back on the Agenda

> 3) High _____.
>
> **5. Future trend**
>
> There is no _____ that China will _____ any time soon.

2.2 Recognizing lecture structure

Several studies have suggested that explicit signals of text structure are important in lecture comprehension. Listening for these signals can therefore help you understand the lecture.

The list below shows some of the most common signals used in lectures to indicate structure. Identifying them in your listening of a lecture greatly enhances your understanding of the structure of the lecture, thus improves your overall mastering of the lecture.

1. Introducing
2. Giving background information
3. Defining
4. Enumerating / Listing
5. Giving examples
6. Showing importance / Emphasizing
7. Clarifying / Explaining / Putting it in other words
8. Moving on / Changing direction
9. Giving further information
10. Giving contrasting information
11. Classifying
12. Digressing
13. Referring to visuals
14. Concluding

Practice 2: Understand a TED lecture. (course audio material 6.2)

Pre-listening brainstorming:

Before you get into the listening of the lecture, think about the topic and brainstorm the following questions.

1. What does the term "birth-control" mean?
2. Do you think that Melinda Gates, the lecturer, will review the history of "birth-control" when saying "let's put birth-control back on the agenda"?
3. According to what you may have known, what is the agenda of birth-control?

Listening for the main idea:

1. Listen to the first part of the lecture and complete the following exercise.
   Birth-control means that:
   1) all men and women should be free to _____;
   2) they should be able to _____;
   3) they have the power to _____.

2. Listen to part of the lecture again and answer the following question.
   What's the attitude of Melinda Gates, the lecturer, towards birth-control?
   _____.

Listening for detailed information:

3. Listen to part of the lecture and complete the following exercise.
   1) Get clear about the following structure by completing the missing information.
      Topic: Birth-control generates public opposition
      Supporting Details: a) Some people _____;
                         b) Some people _____;
                         c) Some people _____.
      Conclusion: These side issues attached to the core idea that _____
      _____.

   2) Who are the victims of this paralysis?

Unit Six Let's Put Birth Control Back on the Agenda

3) How sharp is the contrast of the proportion of people who use contraception?

4) What's the purpose of Melinda Gates' citing the example of Senegal?
   A) To point out the poor condition of birth control in Senegal.
   B) To awaken people that we are not clear about our agenda.
   C) To illustrate the huge gap of birth control in Germany and Senegal.
   D) To address the importance of providing everyone access to birth-control methods.

4. Listen to the part of examples of Melinda Gates and women in Nairobi, and then answer the following questions.
   1) Sum up the family situation of Melinda and Bill Gates, figure out why their children are spaced 3 years apart.

   2) Compare the example of Melinda Gates and women in Nairobi, figure out the similarities between them.

5. Listen to the part of the lecture on smaller size of families, and then complete the following exercise.
Definitely, Melinda Gates disagrees with the coercive policy to bring down family size. Try to pick out the negative words she uses in her lecture to strengthen her disapproval.
   1) Some family planning programs resorted to _____ incentives and coercive policies.
   2) For decades in the United States, African American women were sterilized _____. The procedure was so common, it became known as the Mississippi Appendectomy, a _____ chapter in my country's history.
   3) In Peru, women from the Andes region were given anesthesia and they were sterilized _____.
   4) _____ about this is that these coercive policies weren't even needed.

Listening for the ending:

6. *To end her lecture, Melinda Gates provides a successful example of Bangladesh and pictures a bright future for sub-Saharan Africa. Listen to this part and complete the following exercise.*

1) The successful example of Bangladesh

The Practice: Half the villagers were chosen to _____.

The successful effects: They had a better quality of life than their neighbors 20 years later.

        a) The families: _____;

        b) The women: _____;

        c) The children: _____.

Tips for speaking:

Just the word "lecture" is enough to elicit groans from most people. Nonetheless, there is no reason a lecture needs to be dry and boring or hard to follow. With a few tips, techniques and some practice, just about anyone can give a good lecture on just about any topic.

- Grab your audience's attention. Open with a catchy quote, surprising fact or anecdote that the audience members can relate to.
- Introduce yourself and briefly state what you have to offer your audience—what qualifies you to be here speaking.
- Progress through your lecture smoothly, beginning with your introduction and flowing through your notes to the conclusion. Connect all ideas and examples.
- Maintain eye-contact with your audience members. Scan the audience slowly, so that each audience member feels as if you are addressing him individually.
- Speak clearly. Enunciate your words. Use good grammar. Project to reach the back of the venue, or use a microphone.
- Ask your audience for any questions or comments following your lecture.
- Thank your audience for coming to hear you speak.

Unit Six Let's Put Birth Control Back on the Agenda

Part III Micro-Skills: Common Expressions in Lectures

3.1 Lecture language

Good lectures will contain lots of signs and signals (signposting language) to help you to follow what is being said. Some of these signaling phrases are indicated in the table below.

These are only a few of the many signaling devices that can be used and the table is very simplified — there will be many other phrases that you will discover in the lectures you attend.

Stage of lecture	Purpose of stage	Typical signals
Introduction	• to set the scene • to make sure that the students know what they are going to listen to • to provide other additional materials • to check on general administration matters	OK everyone. Right. Shall we make a start then? Before we get going, can I just ask if everyone has handed in their option forms for next term? Has everyone got a copy of the handout? What I'd like to do today is ... OK everyone, today, we're going to look at ... OK, the focus of today's lecture is on ... I'm going to divide the lecture into three parts ...
Main part of lecture	• to provide demonstrations • to give working examples • to compare and contrast theories	Asking a rhetorical question for emphasis: "So, what is the best way to conserve energy?" Providing additional information: "Another example of this phenomenon is ..."; "We can see this situation elsewhere." Providing a sequence: "Firstly," "Secondly," "Thirdly," etc.

Main part of lecture	• to analyse varying viewpoints • to trace a historical development • to present facts and figures, etc. It is of course impossible to list all the possible functions of a lecture, but the sample marker phrases that you see in the right hand column may occur, regardless of the purpose.	**Referring to sources:** "As Pascal observed, many years ago, ..."; "This is substantiated by Sartre's view of existentialism." **Signalling a shift in the argument:** "Let's turn our attention now to ..."; "What I'd like to do now is to move on to consider ..." **Giving examples:** "For example"; "Let us take the case of ..."; "... is a case in point."; "Let's look particularly at the case of ..." **Emphasising a point:** "The main point I'd like to emphasise here is ..."; "The key issue at stake here is ..."; "What I am essentially arguing is ..." **Providing a digression** (A digression is **not** an important point but is often designed to inject humour or interest into a lecture): "Some of you might just be interested to know that ..."; "You don't need to write this down." **Providing a summary:** "So what I have essentially been doing is ..."; "So the key point to bear in mind is ..." **Referring back to a previous lecture:** "Some of you may remember that in the last lecture, we talked about ..."
Conclusion	• to draw the lecture to a close • to provide a summary of what has been said (if this has not occurred previously in the lecture) • to signal the end	Well, that more or less wraps things up for today. Ok, I think I'll leave it there for today. That's probably about all we've got time for today. Next week, I'd like to go on with this. I'll be looking at ....

Unit Six Let's Put Birth Control Back on the Agenda

Read the following excerpt of a lecture and pay attention to the signals.

Marketing is a process that involves many strategies and activities. **Today, I'm only going to talk about** two parts—product and pricing.

The first thing a business needs to decide is exactly what product, service, or idea its customers want to purchase. To do this, businesses need to determine their target market, **in other words**, who will buy their product. Once a business understands the target market, it can develop its product to fit what the target market will buy. **Second**, after a business has developed a product, it must decide how to price it. If a product is too expensive, consumers won't purchase it. If it is too cheap, the business won't make a profit, and it won't make any money.

Practice 3: Listen for common lecture language. (course audio material 6.3)

1. _____. 2. _____ about some different perspectives on defining and measuring intelligence in adults, and 3 _____.
4 _____, psychologists have generally defined and thought about intelligence as a single quality or level of ability, and that it's possible to measure this ability, like with IQ tests, and compare the levels of general intelligence in people. However, a lot of psychologists who study intelligence actually find it more useful to look at intelligence as divided into distinct capabilities that work together. There are quite a few theories on how to categorize these different capabilities, but 5 _____
_____.

Part IV Recycling

4.1 Building your vocabulary

These are the 10 key vocabulary words and phrases for this unit. Read them, discuss their meanings.

| contraception | transform | abort | sterilize | rein in |
| explosive | gender imbalance | stock out | prior | controversial |

Practice 4: *Complete the following sentences with some of the above key words or phrases. Change the forms if it is necessary.*

1. The cost of the Americans on the Valentine's Day alone can offer all women in Africa free _____ measures for 3 years.
2. It is of top _____ to maintain a sustainable development.
3. Belgium is set to embark on a radical plan to _____ most cats in the country by 2016, which helps to solve the problem of feline overpopulation.
4. It has long been viewed as illegal to check the gender of the fetus and turn to sex-selective _____.
5. This is a _____ experience for people who trace their ancestry. It causes them to look at their lives and define themselves in different ways.

4.2 Strengthening your skills

Group Work: A Research Report on Global Population Issues

Global Population Issues

Goals of the project

Action goals of the project:

- We will make an academic research and report on the topic of "Populations Issues";

Unit Six Let's Put Birth Control Back on the Agenda

- We will divide the class into smaller groups of 5~6 members and a group leader will be elected to be responsible for the smooth progression of the project;
- We will allocate our tasks to each different group member, who will be responsible for specific tasks and finally work together to complete the entire project;
- We will work within groups to narrow down the topic, collect data, make interviews and hold discussions so as to complete the project;
- We will deliver an academic report revealing the findings of our research with visual assistance of PPT presentation or videos, if necessary. Each group member will be responsible for the delivery of his/her own part.

Language goals of the project:
- We will use English to organize the project;
- We will learn to use English to write the script;
- We will use English to deliver the speech in a clear, accurate, appropriate and effective way;
- We will improve our speaking skills through rehearsing the speech.

		Project Schedule	
Step 1	Input	Introduction	
		Preparations for the project	How to plan the project
			How to allocate the task
			Samples
Step 2	Discussion	Narrow down the topic to specific areas that is within our handle and interesting or instructive to the audience.	
		Decide on the roles • Who will be the group leader; • Which part will be allocated to different members; • Who will be responsible for the script; • Who will be responsible for the PPT making;	

		• Who will prepare the videos, if necessary; • Who will shoot the videos.
		Decide on the report • How long should the speech last; • How to seek attention in the introduction; • How to convince your audience that their actions have significant impact on the environment; • How to reinforce your ideas in the conclusion; • How to interact with the audience.
Step 3	Mid-term Report	Report your plan to the teacher and improve your project.
Step 4	Carry out the plan	Collect data and make interviews about the topic; Write down the script; Improve the script with the help of the teacher.
		Each member of the report gets familiar with his/her lines.
		Rehearse the speech. Examine the roles of visual aids and non-verbal language (voice, body language) in making the report.
Step 5	Performance	Deliver the speech in class. Peers evaluation and feedback from the teacher.

《普通学术英语教程:听说与思考》

尊敬的老师:

您好!

为了方便您更好地使用本教材,获得最佳教学效果,我们特向使用本书作为教材的教师赠送本教材配套参考资料。如有需要,请完整填写"教师联系表"并加盖所在单位系(院)公章,免费向出版社索取。

北京大学出版社

教 师 联 系 表

教材名称	《普通学术英语教程:听说与思考》					
姓名:		性别:		职务:		职称:
E-mail:		联系电话:			邮政编码:	
供职学校:			所在院系:			(章)
学校地址:						
教学科目与年级:			班级人数:			
通信地址:						

填写完毕后,请将此表邮寄给我们,我们将为您免费寄送本教材配套资料,谢谢!

北京市海淀区成府路205号　　　　　　　邮 购 部 电话:010-62534449
北京大学出版社外语编辑部　　黄瑞明　　市场营销部电话:010-62750672
邮政编码:100871　　　　　　　　　　　外语编辑部电话:010-62754382
电子邮箱:janette-huang@vip.sina.com